Developments in
Public Employee Relations:
- ## Legislative
- ## Judicial
- ## Administrative

Edited by | **KENNETH O. WARNER**
Executive Director
Public Personnel Association

PUBLIC PERSONNEL ASSOCIATION

1313 East 60th Street   Chicago, Illinois 60637

Foreword

In the early 1940's a committee of experienced administrators presented their pooled opinions about the way government managers and employees should deal with each other. Their book, Employee Relations in the Public Service, published by the Public Personnel Association, became the guidebook on this phase of personnel administration for federal, state, and local government. The theories the committee advanced were widely accepted, and the procedures it recommended were widely adopted.

Where human relations are concerned, however, nothing should ever be considered "settled." Concepts and assumptions can become outmoded; new experience may reveal they were fallacious.

A principal activity of the Public Personnel Association is to provide public administrators with up-to-date knowledge and advice about all the personnel matters that affect their ability to manage. This is a continuing process that is carried out by training institutes, seminars, and conferences, and the publication of a professional journal, Public Personnel Review. From time to time, however, PPA tries to reassess the collection of technical and behavioral formulas that grow up around a particular aspect of public personnel administration—job classification, pay setting, testing, and so on.

In 1960, the Association decided that the time had come for a thorough reappraisal of management-employee relations—as practiced and defended—criticized and advocated. Probably no other phase of personnel administration, in both business and government, has been more affected by the political, economic, social, and psychological changes that have occurred since World War II.

The first new PPA studies of management-employee relations were conducted by two of its chapters, one in Canada and one in the United States. The Vancouver, British Columbia, Metropolitan Chapter reported on the joint efforts of public agencies in the Vancouver area to deal collectively with unions. The San Francisco Bay Area Chapter prepared a report on the status of collective bargaining in the U. S. public service.

In 1963, the Public Personnel Association published a monograph entitled Management Relations with Organized Public Employees: Theory, Policies, Programs. This study tried to provide a background picture of the climate for cooperation by examining the attitudes and concepts held by management, employees, and unions. Other sections described and tried to evaluate different types of management-employee relations programs. Examples of laws, policy statements, and agreements governing management-employee relations were provided.

This second monograph, Developments in Public Employee Relations: Legislative, Judicial, Administrative, published two years later, is an effort to shed further light on the complexities of dealing with employees. It illustrates PPA's continuing effort to encourage innovations in methods in order to solve problems. Sound management-employee relations won't "just happen." They require a positive philosophy, a concerted effort, and a well-organized plan of procedure.

All but two of the contributors to this monograph participated in an Institute on Management-Employee Relations in the Public Service, held in mid-July, 1964, that was sponsored jointly by the International City Managers' Association and the Public Personnel Association. The purpose of the Institute was to help public officials broaden their knowledge and skill in the many facets of employee relations so they would be better equipped to shape plans and policies to fit their particular operating environment.

The five-day Institute program was designed to be a two-way learning process. Papers were prepared in advance by outstanding authorities and practitioners in employee relations. Their lectures were then interspersed with informal discussions, question-and-answer periods, and workshops on practical problems.

This publication presents the results of this two-way learning process. Authors have revised their statements where necessary to reflect the questions asked by participants and to cover the subject more effectively.

This monograph will not provide pat answers or prevent mistakes, but I feel confident that it can help management listen to dissent with an open mind and encourage independent thought and action.

A point made in the preface to Management Relations with Organized Employees needs to be repeated here. The editor and authors accept sole responsibility for the facts and opinions—stated or implied. PPA does not take an official stand on dealing with government employees—organized or unorganized. Varied legal, administrative, and political arrangements govern the hundreds of public personnel agencies that make up the Public Personnel Association. This diversity makes one "right" answer impossible, but it increases the need to share knowledge so that each responsible official can identify the factors he should take into account in making a decision for his own agency.

On behalf of the Public Personnel Association, I thank the men and women who prepared the papers reproduced as chapters in this monograph. All of them had to take time from important professional responsibilities to make this contribution to the literature about public personnel administration. I extend my personal special appreciation to Mrs. Eleanor R. Batson for her assistance in editing the manuscript for publication. Mrs. Batson, former Director of Publications for PPA, is now a free lance writer and editor. I also wish to thank Miss Ruth Smith of our editorial staff for seeing the manuscript through the press.

Chicago   Kenneth O. Warner
March, 1965   Editor

Table of Contents

1.

Employee Attitudes Toward Work, Management, and Unions

Richard M. Lyon

Sir Charles P. Snow, in a stimulating essay entitled "Intellectuals as Natural Luddites" made this arresting observation:

"The industrial revolution looked very different according to whether one saw it from above or below."

Sir Charles admitted that nothing but the industrial revolution could have spread such benefits as health, food, and education "right down to the very poor." But then he paused and asked:

"They [the gains] are the base of our social hope. And yet: do we understand how they have happened? Have we begun to comprehend even the old industrial revolution? Much less the new scientific revolution in which we stand?"

This being 1964 it is too late to worry whether we have understood the old industrial revolution. But a new industrial revolution is upon us, along with the new scientific revolution of which C. P. Snow speaks. We must not fail to understand these two new revolutions just because they, like the old one, still look very different according to whether they are experienced from above or below.

It is my purpose here to discuss the employee view of the employment relationship. I will also try to determine the relevance of this employee viewpoint to the new industrial revolution. To do this, I will (1) set forth some of the essentials of the employment relationship; (2) discuss how the employee perceives this relationship, (3) compare the employee viewpoint with the viewpoint of the employer, and (4) make some recommendations based upon the findings.

The Employer-Employee Relationship

Work and employment is the foundation stone of the industrial process, and the employer-employee relationship, in my opinion, implies conflict—at least for those employees who do not identify themselves with their managers.

I should hasten to explain that, even though I have an obvious economic interest in conflict, it is not my legal training or occupation which leads me to assert that employment implies conflict.

1

Rather, my assertion is the product of my exposure to social science and to the daily realities of industrial relations.

Two Cultures of Industrial America

Conflicts of interest in industry are the key to an understanding of the employment relationship, and I propose to develop this theme around the concept of the two cultures of industrial America. This concept differs from "the two cultures" of C. P. Snow; it is, however, deeply ingrained in our social history.

I will name the American cultures:the culture of scarcity, and the culture of abundance. The culture of scarcity is a culture of pessimism; the culture of abundance is a culture of optimism. The former is the framework of the "manualist," or wage earner, the latter belongs to the business entrepreneur.

This dichotomy on the American industrial scene was first described by the late Selig Perlman, one of this country's most eminent labor historians, in these words:

> "In an economic community there is a separation between those who prefer a secure, though modest return—that is to say, a mere livelihood, and those who play for big stakes and are willing to assume risks in proportion."

The first group includes the great bulk of manual workers. The second group consists of risk takers, the entrepreneurs and businessmen. The manual worker's outlook—fashioned by experience—is that of a world of limited opportunity. The businessman is the eternal optimist to whom the world is brimful of opportunities to be made his own. Scarcity consciousness typical of the manual worker versus the consciousness of abundance motivating the self-confident businessman.

Although Perlman's contribution to the psychology of economic groups, a psychology shaped by perceived economic opportunity, was made a year before the boom broke in 1929, his observations seem to have survived and outlived the crash.

Conflict Over Job Security

To this day organized labor is rooted in a pervasive pessimism premised upon paucity of opportunity for the industrial wage earner. In this culture of pessimism you find the only true explanation for featherbedding and restrictive work practices; for the tremendous fear of displacement by automation which haunts the union leadership today; and, of course, here is the key also to union opposition to subcontracting and to plant relocation. The continued insistence

2

by unions on seniority as a factor in promotion, layoffs, and recalls is still another facet of the culture of pessimism.

In the commitment to seniority, unions often encourage reliance by workers on a most delusive guarantee of security. Length of service in a job is a meaningless yardstick in the face of wholesale displacement of workers when a plant shuts down or when sophisticated machines replace redundant men. In 1962 the President's Advisory Committee on Labor Management Policy called for the "recognition by unions, individual employees, and employers of the necessity of adapting seniority and other rules in order to facilitate mobility of workers, while providing for the equities of employees." The Studebaker shutdown experience, for example, makes one wonder why unions would not be willing—even glad—to make changes in seniority rules. There, if you will recall, senior workers were eventually discharged after the younger men had at least been given advance time to comb South Bend for jobs. The older workers finally realized the irony of their so-called "security." When the UAW was able to negotiate jobs for 50 men in Swedish automobile plants, the union was asked to refer only young, unencumbered men!

The conflict over job security has become one point of collision for the two cultures. Equally significant to an understanding of the employee view of employment is a conflict that might be described as personal security. It stems from the demands the organization makes on the individual.

Conflict Over Personal Security

Increasing attention has been directed in recent years to organizational behavior. Apparently, as organization increases so does human resistance to it. The needs of healthy individuals tend to be incompatible with the demands of the organizations of which they are a part. The total identification of man and organization, given popular exposure in William H. Whyte's book, The Organization Man, does not seem to operate at the nonmanagerial level. On the contrary, the worker develops elaborate behavior patterns to accommodate the needs of the organization, rather than be absorbed by the organization. Important among these behavior patterns is the creation of secondary associations to serve as psychological shelters from the demands of the organization. The secondary associations can, of course, provide the means to influence the primary work-centered association. Unions are but one such psychological shelter.

As our understanding of conflict on both levels has increased, we have learned to view conflict—within limits—as beneficial to the participants. Over the years we have found the means to accommodate and reconcile seemingly irreconcilable opposites within a broad sphere of agreement.

The consequences of conflict have led the hourly worker to form and join unions, particularly since the passage of the Wagner Act in 1935. In brief, workers have joined unions because of two beliefs: (1) only collectively can they assert mastery over job opportunities and obtain job security; and (2) only collectively can they assert their individuality at work.

Four questions must be asked to assess the employee view of employment:

1. What does work mean to the employee?

2. What does the enterprise mean to the employee?

3. What does the union mean to the employee?

4. How does the employee see himself?

Employee Attitude Toward Work

Sigmund Freud once stated that most people "work only when forced by necessity," and he was satisfied that "this natural human aversion to work gives rise to the most difficult social problem." But, Ferdynand Zweig, in his book, The Worker in an Affluent Society, makes the intriguing and probably truer observation that the "attitude to work is the most complex of all a man's attitudes, often involving not only strong ambivalence but also side thrusts in all directions. . . ." Zweig links the personal attitude to work to such factors as temperament, character, age, health, life experience, marital status, skill, nature of work, wages and working conditions, industry and place of work, and fellow workers.

Research shows, for example, that unlike skilled manual workers, the unskilled or semiskilled are more likely to engage in restriction of output and in similar reactions to inherently dull and repetitive tasks, largely beyond the control of the operator.

Eric Hoffer, the articulate and thoughtful longshoreman-philosopher, distinguished between finding fulfillment in work and finding justification in it. Since Hoffer worked with his hands all of his life, as a migratory field worker before serving as a longshoreman for the past 20 years, his observations on work certainly deserve attention.

"No one will claim that the majority of people in the Western World, be they workers or managers, find fulfillment in their work. But they do find in it a justification of their existence. The paycheck and the profitable balance sheet are certificates of value. Where the job requires exceptional skill or tests a person's capacities there is an additional sense of exhilaration.

"The remarkable thing is that the Occident's addiction to work is by no means synonymous with love of work. The Western workingman actually has the illusion that he can kill work and be done with it. He 'attacks' every job he undertakes and feels the ending of a task as a victory."

The task may have been completed, but its repetition is the basis for the factory system. It comes, therefore, as no surprise that when the Industrial Relations Center of the University of Chicago summarized ten years of attitude measurements it found that one-third of the American workers are apathetic and indifferent about their work. Another research study involving 4,300 production workers in 14 companies revealed that the feelings and attitudes of production workers towards their work situation is at best lukewarm. Still another study reported that three out of four employees do not consider their jobs and work places as central life interests for themselves.

Employee Attitude Toward the Place of Work

Eric Hoffer has suggested that the place of work is not viewed differently from work itself.

"The awareness of being an eternal workingman colors one's attitudes.

"To the eternal workingman management is substantially the same whether it is made up of profit seekers, idealists, technicians, or bureaucrats. The allegiance of the manager is to the task and the results. However noble his motives, he cannot help viewing the workers as a means to an end. He will always try to get the utmost out of them; and it matters not whether he does it for the sake of profit, for a holy cause, or for the sheer principle of efficiency.

"One need not view management as an enemy or feel self-righteous about doing an honest day's work to realize that things are likely to get tough when management can take the worker for granted; when it can plan and operate without having to worry about what the worker will say or do."

Employee Attitude Toward the Union

The appeal of the union is twofold. Since work is a necessary evil, collective action can protect jobs, assure adequate pay, and prevent arbitrary treatment by the employer. Union action is perceived as an expression of independence from management control for the purpose of gaining greater control over the conditions of work, if necessary, through the imposition of restrictions on the formal authority of management.

Unions Lose Members and Strength

Judged by current statistics, union popularity must give the labor leadership some cause for concern. Between 1960 and 1962, unions reported a net decline of close to one-half million members.

After a spectacular increase in membership between 1936 and 1944, unions continued to grow to a peak of 17.5 million in 1956. Since then, the figure has gone down by one million. The Bureau of Labor Statistics further reports that the loss in absolute numbers has been accompanied by a decline in the relative strength of the labor movement as a proportion of the total labor force. Only one out of five employees is a union member. In nonagricultural establishments the ratio has dropped to three out of ten. Among the unions showing declines were those in communications, metal working, mining, and textiles. Increases were reported by unions in government service, air and sea transportation, retail trade, and service occupations and also by those unions that have jurisdiction over skilled workers.

The decline in the percentage of union members is due, in part, to the fact that since 1956 white-collar employment in this country has for the first time surpassed blue-collar employment. This, however, is only a partial explanation. Massive layoffs in steel and other technologically changing industries affect union membership statistics. Close to one-half million manufacturing jobs have disappeared in the last five or six years. Worker disenchantment with the unions has accompanied the transformation of organized labor from a movement to an institution.

Rapport Between Worker and Union Declines

The growing complexities of business also have rubbed off on the union organizational structure and on the union outlook. On a personal level, the widening gap between management and worker has found its counterpart in the loss of personal ties between the worker and his union. In the days of Sam Gompers you would not have heard a union man complain: "What I need is a union to represent me to my union." You do hear this complaint today. Professor Paul Sultan has written a book, The Disenchanted Unionist, about the lost, discontented union members, who are too perplexed to be called rebels. Sultan concludes:

> "It is clear that union leaders have lost much of the intimacy with, and understanding for, their own membership. Ideologically and emotionally, the member's attachment to his union has become increasingly impersonal, if not superficial."

Unions Lack Imaginative Leadership

The unions may well have organized some of the unorganized, but they have failed to unionize them. The same message is reflected in the recent writings of Paul Jacobs, B. J. Widick, Sidney Lens, and Solomon Barkin. Most of these men are disappointed—if not disenchanted—unionists. They all seem to agree on this: Imaginative ladership is lacking; new ideas have not been in evidence for a long time, and the big problems like unemployment, automation, and equal employment opportunities, cannot be adequately solved by collective bargaining as now constituted. It is precisely these big problems which haunt the leadership.

The March, 1964, issue of the Labor Law Journal contained an article by Solomon Barkin and Albert A. Blum titled "What's To Be Done for Labor? The Trade Unionist's Answer." The article reported results of a survey of 38 union presidents and 47 union staff members. The authors—both men with union sympathies—concluded that the proposals for action put forth by the union presidents and staff are "vague and general and provide no blueprints for plans. They certainly do not reflect intensive debate, thought or planning."

What steps do these leaders propose to improve matters from the union viewpoint? Barkin and Blum report that the most frequently mentioned is better government and legislation through political action. Next in line after political action, the survey indicates union leadership preference for internal organizational reforms, better union education programs, and for more effective and new organizing.

Possible Impact of Technological Changes

Those findings are most interesting when you consider that unlike the European picture the political appeal of U.S. unions is very limited. "Class consciousness" has not featured strongly as a reason for union membership in the United States. Union political influence may well be on the upswing as automation accelerates and occupational obsolescence proceeds.

The potential political consequences of technological change are explosive yet are too often ignored by those who assess social problems against market standards. A prominent bank, for example, recently went on record saying that it might be cheaper to give the unemployable a grant of $3,000 a year rather than try to create jobs for them by resorting to policies risking inflation. Much of the criticism of the poverty program proposed by the Johnson Administration had a similarly hollow ring. Insofar as the problem affects the Negro, one can readily agree with Professor Arnold R. Weber of the University of Chicago, who declared that the Negro drive for economic and social equality probably owes as much to automation as to Dr. Martin Luther King.

The problem is, of course, not limited to the Negro. Professor John C. Leggett of the University of California reported that there are signs that persistent economic insecurity and uprootedness give rise to class consciousness which sometimes engenders collective protests demanding the amelioration of the conditions of the uprooted worker. These protests, in turn, function so as to strengthen the class consciousness of the uprooted, especially those who both derive from rural backgrounds and presently belong to labor unions. These "uprooted" workers are found to express a higher level of class consciousness than do "settled" workers, partially because the uprooted bring with them fewer skills and experiences that might help them to deal effectively with the industrial environment.

Professor Leggett also reported that the unemployed are most class conscious than those with work. A considerably higher percentage of unemployed workers are either militant egalitarians (who believe in reallocating wealth on an equal basis) or militant radicals. The one exception to this are unemployed Negroes who appear slightly less class conscious than the employed Negroes. Negroes without work, seemingly, do not acquire unusually militant class perspectives unless they belong to unions.

Prospects for New Union Growth

My own experience as a management adviser leads me to conclude that prospects for an upturn in union membership are remote.

In preparation for this discussion, I reviewed the handouts of several unions in recent organization campaigns in the Chicago area. The handbills—apart from outright falsities and misstatements concerning the employers' working conditions, the management, and working conditions elsewhere—contained very few, if any, good reasons why the employees would be better off by joining the union, other than that the union would henceforth deal directly with the employer and obtain vast improvements in cash and fringe benefits.

The organizers, even though assisted by in-plant volunteers, showed generally a poor acquaintance with the real conditions at work, and not once did they relate themselves or their union to the labor movement as a whole. Evidently, it takes action from companies like Kohler and Essex Wire to fire up organized labor! The old men who are the national union leaders seemingly prefer to talk about political action.

This is not to deny that unions must be credited with signal contributions to the development of "law of the shop." "The American worker has certain rights by virtue of his history; others, as a consequence of his citizenship; and still others, because of his membership in a trade union." So said Professors Eli Ginsberg and Ivan E. Berg in their interesting little volume entitled <u>Democratic Values and the Rights of Management</u>.

Clearly unions have been able to affect the rights of management by enhancing the rights of the workers. However, Professors Ginzberg and Berg believe that the most substantial accomplishment of the union in labor-management relations has been the development of the grievance procedure in the collectively bargained agreement for the control, reduction, and peaceful solution of conflict.

"While the union has acted to protect the worker in a great many different ways, not only in the work arena directly but also out of it, no other accomplishment exceeds in importance what it has been able to achieve through the development of a formal system for the adjudication of grievances at the work place. The difference between the free man and the serf is the difference in the rights of each to plan and control his life. And since work fills so much of a man's life, his opportunity to enhance his freedom is through acquiring ever larger control over the conditions under which he works."

Only a maturing of organized labor made possible the maturing of labor-management relations. Yet this same maturing or organized labor is accompanied by growing structural and operational rigidities which discourage new departures. This is most clearly noticeable in the union's lack of success in organizing white collar workers. B. C. Roberts, a British observer, expressed it this way:

"Unions are not likely to secure their allegiance . . . so long as they consider white collar employees to be simply blue collar employees with bleached shirts," and we may add, "or skirts."

The late Albert Camus, viewing the European scene, wrote some 10 years ago:

"There is no dearth of opportunities for action. . . . Trade unionism is today the first, and the most fruitful among them."

Judged by their deeds, few American union leaders would seem to concur.

The Employee View of Himself

Eli Chinoy in his book <u>Automobile Workers and the American Dream</u> contrasts the traditional American success-oriented theory of life with the realities that confront the assembly-line worker and his family:

"The tradition of opportunity imposes heavy burdens upon workers who must repeatedly reconcile desire, stimulated from diverse sources—with the realities of working class life. Since each individual is assigned full responsibility for his economic fate, failure can be due only to limited ability or defects in character—lack of ambition or determination or initiative, for example—and not to the absence of opportunity."

The underlying assumption that Chinoy finds many workers making about themselves is that failure to rise from the level of wage labor is one's own fault. This assumption is not realistic, but it is more likely to be accepted than questioned.

Erich Fromm provides us with this self-portrait of the industrial worker in the age of the machine:

"He spends his best energy for seven or eight hours a day in producing 'something.' He needs his work in order to make a living, but his role is essentially a passive one. He fulfills a small isolated function in a complicated and highly organized process of production, and is never confronted with 'his' product as a whole, at least not as a producer, but only as a consumer, provided he has the money to buy 'his' product in a store. He is concerned neither with the whole product in its physical aspects nor with its wider economic and social aspects. He is put in a certain place, has to carry out a certain task, but does not participate in the organization or management of the work. He is not interested, nor does he know why one produces this instead of another commodity—what relation it has to the needs of society as a whole. The shoes, the cars, the electric bulbs, are produced by 'the enterprise' using the machines. He is part of the machine, rather than its master as an active agent. The machine, instead of being in his service to do work for him which once had to be performed by sheer physical energy, has become his master. Instead of the machine being the substitute for human energy, man has be-

come a substitute for the machine. His work can be defined as
the performance of acts which cannot yet be performed by machines."

Under these circumstances getting ahead means in the words
of a machine operator with ten years' seniority "working up to a
job where you don't get kicked around." Advancement on the job becomes less important than security on the job. Automobile workers
prefer a steady job over one that is not steady, even if the latter
pays higher wages. The achievement of security is the essence of
advancement. Advancement is also redefined by including goals and
interests unrelated to the job, typically by defining success in terms
of the acquisition of material goods and of a home, and by projecting
the worker's hopes on his children. Unhappily, the worker's adaption
to the work situation through goldbricking, apathy, and withholding
of production cannot help but rub off on the children. A depth study
of working class boys in late adolescence confirms that the boys
learned to view the occupational system from their parents' perspective. From this and other research, Chris Argyris listed the
following six attitudes the child would typically pick up:

1. Don't expect "happiness" on the job.

2. Leave it if you don't like it.

3. "Take" the frustration and work hard to become a member
of management.

4. Or play it smart; join the union; gain seniority. Don't work
too hard; don't work too little. Keep in the middle.

5. Once you have the seniority take it easy. Listen to the old
timers. They'll show you the ropes.

6. Make as much money as you can.

Wight Bakke noted that many working class parents sought to
provide their children with enough education to avoid a working
class life. The children shared this desire but often they simply
cannot bear the frustration which prolonged education requires.

The Employer View of Employment

Time does not permit giving equal time to the employer's view
of the employment relationship. This viewpoint ranges from unlim-
ited fear of employee invasion of the God-given rights of management to an almost missionary zeal for making work fun.

I detect that the management-rights-centered executive is slowly being displaced by the solution-oriented manager who pays less
attention to status and more to results. Any generalization in this

area, however, carries with it its own exceptions. Much depends upon factors such as the experience of the particular enterprise and the perceived, or actual, management philosophy of "the old man."

An example of the newer approaches to management organization and job design is the pronouncement of Edwin H. Land of the Polaroid Corporation:

"Industry should address itself now to the production of a worthwhile, highly rewarding, highly creative, inspiring daily job for every one of a hundred million Americans."

A great deal of research effort has gone into the problems connected with job satisfaction. Today, the people who are responsible for industrial relations have to cope increasingly with motivating employees to work and increasing employee job satisfaction. "The jobs most people do," says Dr. Frederick Herzberg, chairman of the department of psychology at Western Reserve University, "are not a rich source for psychological health, and, in fact, they may often best be classified as mental hazards."

Industry has concentrated most effort on satisfying the economic and social needs of employees. Wage and salary administrators have teamed up with time and motion engineers and have devised a multiplicity of incentive pay programs. Lawyers, actuaries, and bankers have teamed up with industry to provide the bulk of factory workers with benefit programs ranging from pension and disability payments to employer-financed tuition plans and free legal aid. Increasing attention is being directed to the individual psychological needs of workers.

A leading contribution in the field of clincial psychiatry and psychology has been made by Frederick Herzberg, Bernard Mauser, and Barbara Bloch Snyderman. The authors found that two entirely different sets of factors influenced job satisfaction.

Five factors stand out as high determiners of job satisfaction: achievement, recognition, work itself, responsibility, and advancement. Herzberg calls these factors motivators, since they are effective in motivating the individual to superior performance.

A different set of factors is involved in job dissatisfaction. These factors, the dissatisfiers, refer mainly to the job context or job environment. Among these are: the nature of the company's policies and practices, the type of supervision, working conditions of the job, and the pay.

Dissatisfiers appear to have little effect on positive job attitudes; they generally describe the work environment. They are the

12

hygiene factors, analogous with the medical use of this term as preventive and environmental.

The need to avoid unpleasantness expressed itself in the dis-satisfiers; the need for individual growth and meaning is expressed in the motivators.

". . . the effects of hygiene factors on job attitudes are of a relatively short duration in contrast with the motivator factors which, three of them at least [work-responsibility and advancement] have long lasting attitude effects."

Before examining the personnel policy implications of Herzberg's motivational analysis, I want to mention some observations of Victor Frankl, the Viennese psychiatrist, that are most pertinent to the world of work:

". . . mental health is based on a certain degree of tension, the tension between what one has already achieved and what one still ought to accomplish, or the gap between what one is and what one should become. Such a tension is inherent in the human being and therefore is indispensable to mental well-being."

"We should not, then, be hesitant about challenging man with a potential meaning for him to fulfill. . . . What man needs is not a tensionless state but rather the striving and struggling for some goal worthy of him."

The central place of work in man's life is vividly illustrated by this statistic: Over half the people questioned in Dr. Frankl's clinic in Vienna showed themselves to be in a state of boredom. "In actual fact," he noted, "boredom is now causing, and certainly bringing to psychiatrists, more problems to solve than is distress." Frankl sees these problems as growing increasingly crucial as automation enhances the leisure potential.

Granted even the American worship for the active life, it is not entirely unthinkable that the European "Sunday neurosis," the depression that afflicts people who don't know what to do with themselves when the rush of the busy work week is over, may hit us on these shores in the form of a "short work week neurosis." On both sides of the Atlantic there is already evidence in the form of rising crime, delinquency, alcoholism, and even in much aimless driving, that many people do not have worthwhile commitments to give meaning to their lives.

The implications for a new management viewpoint of the employment relationship and for appropriate policies are clear. Fringe benefits—costing billions of dollars—are truly that in name and in fact. They do not motivate, if motivation arises out of the challenge of the job, responsibility, achievement, recognition, and expanding opportunities for advancement.

Conclusion

What I have been trying to demonstrate is that the missing link, the bridge between our two cultures in industrial America, is motivation for work because of the intrinsic nature of the job. I cannot suggest any single way to create this link or bridge. Jobs vary; so do personal capacities, interests and backgrounds.

If there is one area that I would select to begin work to ease the conflict between the two cultures, it would be precisely that of motivation. We should not be discouraged and continue to trod conventional paths simply because motivation is so complex. Just as the "hidden persuaders" have to tap the subconscious in order to sell their products, we may have to tap subconscious areas in the minds of workers and management, with the goal of a socially constructive outcome.

I do not mean at all that we brain-wash or sugar-coat; I mean that we try to find out what is really needed and important to the laboring man's life on the job. This we still do not know. Then we must determine how closely we can fulfill this through our technology and our psychological wisdom.

It would be well for managements and unions both to rethink the directions in which they are now moving—political action and community good works—and reflect their social concerns by attending to life in the factory, the store, and the office.

Specifically, our first task as managers will be to understand what motivates employees; our second task will be to integrate these "motivators" into policies and practices. Until we accomplish these tasks we cannot claim to have even begun to understand the new industrial revolution, its challenges and its dangers.

2. Nature and Purpose of Management Communication

Robert K. Burns

The executive environment is dominated by a continuing, interrelated set of communication flows and activities. My purpose here is to examine this world of words. What is the nature of the communication process? What skills are involved? How can improvement in understanding and performance enhance communication efforts?

Three Aspects of Communication

The process of communication embraces three interrelated domains. The first of these, communication at the level of facts, may be regarded as essentially intellectual in character. Factual communication includes getting and giving of information, providing reasons and explanations, and transmitting orders and instructions. Certainly organization-wide dissemination of facts is integral to effective operation of any agency—public or private.

The second dimension of communication operates at the level of feelings. This emotional component of communication takes into account sentiments, attitudes, and personal orientations. In dealing with difficult situations, it is usually clear that communicating at the factual or informational level is by no means enough. Intellectual problems involved in getting and giving information, understanding, sanction and support cannot effectively be attacked until the emotional feelings and sentiments of individuals are first dealt with. Consequently, it is important to recognize that feelings frequently underlie and help to determine the logical and rational response of individuals in a communication situation. This explains the wisdom of keeping constantly in mind the maxim by the Latin writer Publilius Syrus: "It is easy for men to say one thing and think another."

A third dimension of communication is essentially behavioral in character. It involves communication in terms of actions, reactions, symbols and nonverbal responses. The importance of this facet of communication is succinctly summarized by this admonition of Ralph Waldo Emerson: "Do not say things. What you are stands over you the while, and thunders so that I cannot hear what you say to the contrary."

15

To sum up, total communication effectiveness involves an understanding of all three aspects of communication—intellectual, emotional, behavioral—and their appropriate use with reference to the requirements of the situation.

Maximizing Communication

The indispensable requirement for effective communication in an organization is the belief of those individuals who are in management and supervisory positions that they have an obligation to share information and sentiments about important matters with the people who will be affected by those matters. To be fully effective, of course, this belief must be backed up by official policy.

A second condition for maximizing communication effectiveness is a climate that makes communication and verbal interaction possible. Essentially this requires that management accept each person for what he is, empathize with his point of view, and try to understand his problems. This approach fosters two-way communication. It helps employees understand messages they receive from management and prepare messages to send to management. It has been said that the most beautiful word in the English language is "love"; the second, "help."

A third important condition for maximizing communication is to have open information channels that link all the units in an organization. There must be upward and downward flows of information within a functionally operating unit, sideward flows between units, and outward and inward flows that bridge and link the organization to its publics and its total environment. Only this free interchange can provide full understanding in terms of facts, feelings, and behavior.

Importance of Communication

Communication is the only continuing means by which administrators can successfully influence and affect others in an organization. Indeed, it lies at the core of the administrative process. Management involves managing work, managing men, managing ideas, and managing relations and situations. Since all of these administrative tasks are accomplished through communication, Peter Drucker has concluded that no matter whether the manager's job is engineering, accounting, or selling, his effectiveness depends on his ability to listen, to read, on his ability to speak and to write.

A number of studies have been made of the amount of time that administrators spend communicating. Some show that executives in industry spend up to 75 per cent of their time reading, writing, speaking or listening. The written or "paper work" aspects of the administrator's communication burden consume one-quarter of the time. Approximately 9 per cent is spent in writing and 16 per cent in reading. The oral component of the executive's communication role involves speaking (principally asking or answering) and listening. Approximately 30 per cent of his communication time is spent speaking and 45 per cent in listening.

The total volume of written or paper work aspects of communication seems to be mounting substantially. It has been estimated that a total of 750,000 words, in the form of reports, memoranda, letters, and the like, is piled on a typical corporation president's desk every month. If he read all of this material, it would take approximately five hours a day. This would mean that almost half of his salary would be paid for reading. Obviously this is an impossible demand upon his limited time. A maximum of 25 per cent of a manager's communication time devoted to both the reading and written forms of interchange, as reported above, would seem to be a more reasonable figure. Probably in many companies it could be less.

So far as employees are concerned, it has been estimated that companies spend in excess of $500 million a year in their communication effort. In his survey of executive decisionmaking, M. H. Jones concluded that most companies probably spend more money and man-hours on communication and get less from it per dollar spent than any other single activity.

Despite the difficulties in effecting communication, it must be recognized that communication lies at the heart of both the work and interpersonal relationships in an organization. The hard core of any administrative unit is found in the man-boss relationship, the essence of which, to a substantial degree, stems from communication—particularly the face-to-face, day-to-day, man-to-man oral exchange of information, feelings, actions, and reactions. Communication is essential to motivation and getting work done, and it exercises a pervasive influence on performance of the job in all of its aspects.

Forms and Functions of Communication

The various alternative forms and media of communication have different characteristics and uses. Speaking and writing are ways in which we communicate directly to others. Listening and reading are ways others communicate directly with us. The person who speaks well, writes well, listens well, and reads well tends to communicate well in terms of the audio-verbal forms of expression.

Writing and reading, the written forms of communication, are essentially intellectual in terms of tone and content. They are particularly appropriate for formal, official, and procedural purposes where adequacy, accuracy, and referencing are important. The oral forms of communication, which include speaking and listening, are usually more expressive of feelings and emotions. They are particularly important in lingual and interpersonal relationships and in understanding and dealing with attitudes, sentiments, values, and beliefs. Finally, the behavioral component of communication—nonverbal actions, reactions and responses—have important overtones for operating effectiveness and interpersonal relationships in many situations.

In interpersonal contacts, a combination of all three aspects of communication produces the total impact. For example, findings indicate that people learn and remember 40 per cent of what they hear, 55 per cent of what they see, and 70 per cent of what they hear and see. In other words, combining the audio and visual approaches to communication intensifies the imprinting of the communication message upon the receiver and therefore increases its effectiveness.

Forms and methods of communication should be chosen with regard to the communication objectives one is trying to achieve. The end results of a communication effort can then be evaluated in terms of the accomplishment of one or more purposes. For example, one objective might be essentially informative—to inform others or be informed by them. An alternative objective might be primarily instructive or directive—to give orders and instructions, demonstrate methods or procedures, and observe progress and problems. Still another purpose may be essentially persuasive—to get others to understand, accept, and implement a specific endeavor or plan of action. Finally, communication may be evaluative in its objective—to assess and appraise existing beliefs, policies, procedures, and activities.

Techniques and Skills of Communication

It was pointed out earlier that an important requirement for effective communication is a climate where people are willing, and psychologically able, to communicate with one another. Skill in climate-setting calls for the ability to convey to another individual a basic acceptance of him as a person and of his problems whatever they may be. This requires showing an interest in him and in his problems, making clear a willingness to explore a problem free from bias and judgment, and trying to understand what can be done to help improve his situation.

Skill in establishing a permissive relationship is a first-order requirement for the administrator. When an administrator succeeds, the employee will recognize that he does not have to struggle with his superior but is free to struggle with himself and his own problems. In the last analysis, of course, no one can solve another person's problems. Each person must solve his own. Administrators can, however, create the climate and conditions that will encourage employees to think their way into and through problems and come up with their own solutions. This requires a conviction on the part of management that people have the desire, capacity, and potential for solving their problems if they are given the necessary encouragement and help. Specialists who come to grips with the truly tough interpersonal problems of people, such as clinical psychologists, psychiatrists, and psychoanalysts, recognize the importance of aiding the individual to face up to his own difficulties as a first step in solving them. These experts have long since discarded such traditional techniques as coercion, pressure, and punishment for they have proved to be largely ineffective in helping individuals understand and solve their problems. Indeed, in handling problems involving attitudes, values, beliefs, and behavior, the direct methods leave much to be desired. The indirect methods of understanding, discussing, participating, questioning, and listening are much more effective.

When dealing with attitudes, feelings, and behavior of individuals, more administrators should recognize that asking is frequently much better than telling. Asking enables the questioner to direct communication into new channels that may be more relevant and constructive. Asking also initiates two-way interaction. The power of a question lies in the fact that it compels an answer. The right type of question tends to produce the right kind of answer. There are different types of questions for different purposes. Rudyard Kipling once wrote:

> I keep six honest serving-men
> (They taught me all I knew);
> Their names are What and Why
> and When
> And How and Where and Who.

Questions starting with these words tend to produce answers that not only provide facts as facts but also disclose the feelings of those involved. The listener thus gets a better appreciation of the problem as seen by the speaker, an appreciation that is particularly important in the boss-man relationship. A subordinate usually has information that the boss must have in order to make good judgments. When the subordinate starts speaking, the boss—who asked the right questions then listens—begins to learn. Since different kinds of questions produce different kinds of answers, an effective communicator must first learn how to be an effective questioner.

It is obvious that anyone who asks a question should be pre-pared to listen to the answer. But passive listening is not enough. The listener must actively try to help the other person communi-cate information and feelings. One way to do this is for the listen-er to restate what he has heard. This gives the speaker an oppor-tunity to clear up any misunderstandings. The listener can make various types of neutral responses to show that he is attentive. The listener may want to reflect back the feelings of the speaker if they are heavily oriented emotionally. It may help the speaker to hear how his feelings sound when they are expressed by someone else. By summarizing frequently at natural watersheds in the conversa-tion, the listener can help to break down a problem into manage-able parts that can be analyzed, understood, and given attention.

Learning to discipline oneself and listen understandingly is a difficult skill to acquire. Many managers who operate under the assumption that managers must manage and make decisions feel that inviting ideas and suggestions from others, listening to what they say, letting them participate, is essentially "soft supervision." Usually the opposite is more nearly the case. Only when managers understand a situation fully will they feel sufficiently self-confident and secure to allow others to suggest, recommend, participate, and take responsibility.

Learning how to channel thinking for constructive problem-solving and action is another important communication skill. This skill involves knowing how to define and state an issue in terms of the type of analysis and action required. These requirements may be essentially informational, political, or procedural, or they may be problem-solving in character. If it is information that is needed to solve a problem, the methods and techniques for maximizing the communication of information—in its most meaningful form—over the shortest possible time—must be considered. Handling a policy or procedural issue calls for weighing the relative advantages and disadvantages of alternative courses of action. Solving an unsolved problem involves an analysis of components, causes, action to be taken, who is to do it, and when it is to be completed.

The end objective of most communication is to get people to think together and work together to accomplish certain purposes. It is quite obvious, of course, that the people have to dissipate any feelings of anger, tension, hostility, and aggression before they can think constructively and work cooperatively together. Consequently, in any problem situation it is desirable first to find out how people feel then dispose and drain off any tension, anxiety, and hostility before proceeding to the hard core intellectual discussion and ra-tional consideration of issues and alternatives.

Some Barriers to Communication

Most administrators have, at one time or another, encountered a wide range of barriers to effective communication. One of the most frustrating is the sheer lack of time. However, when administrators recognize that communication is essential to building cooperation and teamwork, they somehow will find time for it. Administrators must also realize that decisionmaking is not complete until communication of the decision has been accomplished. In a sense, therefore, communication is a final requirement to almost every action, and the action in a given situation is not complete until its communication is effected. When communication is good, problems of misunderstanding, primary and secondary follow-up action, the institution of control systems, and the like, become less important. The time saved by eliminating post-factum activities can be used for initial communication.

Even where there is adequate time to communicate with others, barriers and roadblocks tend inevitably to develop. One of these is the fact-inference problem. Frequently, people act upon what they think are reasonable facts and a true understanding of a situation. To others, however, the understanding and action seem to be based upon inferences or assumptions that are invalid. When a problem arises all of the needed facts are seldom available. An "allness" orientation (we have all the needed information; we already know all about the problem; we have already made up our minds), tends greatly to inhibit communication. No one knows everything about anything. There are always additional kinds of information that may have a bearing on a situation or decision. Avoiding allness responses and practices can remove important barriers to much interpersonal communication.

A third roadblock in communication is overcoming problems of meaning. In communicating with others there is always a question of whose meaning is attached to the words that are used. The problem of meaning in what is communicated resides in the persons not in the words. Semanticists insist that words do not mean—people mean. Indeed, the 500 most frequently used words in the English language have over 14,000 different meanings. A writer or speaker should never assume that the meaning he gives to words is necessarily that of the reader or listener. It is important to check for meaning by restating, clarifying, and using similar communication and listening procedures.

Our interpretation and response to communications from others, in terms of what we say and do, may introduce additional difficulties in communication. One of these barriers is known as the "two-valued orientation." This is essentially an either/or approach to interacting and intercommunicating with others. Frequently this reaction takes the form of a polar, rigid and inflexible position or viewpoint. Something is either right or wrong, good or bad, effective or ineffective. Actually, however, there may be many degrees of difference between extremes and many shades and variations in between. When people take rigid and extreme positions they tend to overlook intervening differences and ignore qualifying factors, situations, and alternatives. The response of others to a rigid two-valued viewpoint is usually to suppress communication and to lower an iron curtain between those engaged in the interchange.

Communication takes place through time. And in the process of time all things are in the state of change—problems, people, relationships, and situations. What may be true today may not be true tomorrow. Therefore, in communicating with individuals the need for indexing, dating, and identifying points of time becomes important. Failure to do this often creates confusion, misunderstanding, and disagreement.

Perhaps the most important barrier in communication is the failure to recognize the responsibility for helping the other person communicate. Communication is a two-way, participating process. Each of us should try to help the other person get his ideas across to us. It is as important as trying our utmost to communicate our ideas to him. Once again, the key is patience, empathy, and a desire to understand and help. If these requirements are clearly established, some of the difficulties of communication diminish because the basis for an effective two-way interchange becomes clear and evident.

3.

Management's Right to Manage

William Hotchkiss

This issue is not a simple one nor is it resolved either in the
public sector or in private industry. It is not a new issue. Back in
1945 President Truman convened a national labor-management conference with top leaders from the union movement and from industry, to make an assessment of collective bargaining. That particular conference foundered on this very issue of management's right
to manage.

Because the members of that committee—both management and
labor—could not agree on what management's rights were, the management members submitted their own report. Here is the introduc-
tory paragraph of that report:

"Labor members of the committee on management's right to
manage have been unwilling to agree on any listing of specific management functions. Management members of the committee conclude,
therefore, that labor members are convinced that the field of collective bargaining will, in all probability, continue to expand into the
field of management. The only possible end of such a philosophy
would be a joint management of enterprise, and to this the management members naturally cannot agree."

What Is Management's Function?

The management members went on to state what they thought
management functions were, and listed those functions which were
solely management's responsibility. Nearly 20 years later, the issue still is not resolved. It is still on collective bargaining tables
all over the country.

The Wall Street Journal ran a story recently on the auto negotiations, with a headline about "a long hot summer." The sub-head-
line was, "Who is going to run the plants?" When matters of principle are being discussed—management rights and union rights—
there is no easy compromise.

"Management Prerogatives"

Leonard Woodcock, who is head of the GM department of the
UAW, and a guest columnist for the Detroit News, wrote an article

23

called "Management Prerogative Is a Matter of Semantics." He says the phrase "management prerogatives"—not "rights," but prerogatives—is like the "other semantic classics which have been used to anaesthetize intelligent examination of the relations between employers and employees in this country. . . ."

He continues: "Furthermore, that as management the people in control have specified, exactly determined rights, which either arise out of the natural order, suggesting a kind of social Darwinism, or out of a divinely given rule, or out of a racial memory through the common law, or perhaps rights which are enumerated in the Magna Carta, the Declaration of Independence, the Articles of Confederation, the Bill of Rights, the Emancipation Proclamation, and, of course, and especially, the Fifth and 14th amendments to the Constitution."

He obviously is poking fun at it, but he is deadly serious. To conclude he says: "Collective bargaining exists as a national policy precisely because human beings have paramount rights which cannot be ground under so-called prerogative. Most of the words of a management-union agreement concern themselves with limitations of what otherwise have been described as 'management prerogative.'"

Dealing with the Automation Problem

At a recent meeting on automation discussion focussed on how to handle automation. How does management deal with employee displacement? How much consultation does management do? Does the union help? Do you plan jointly with them? Do you inform them? Or do you do it unilaterally?

There were, of course, all kinds of answers. In some areas management did a great deal of joint planning with the union. But it is ironic that the stickiest issue of all—the issue of jobs, or assignment of employees to work—is the issue that's now paramount in most collective bargaining situations.

Past Practices vs. Adapting to Change

Does management have the right to go back and change work practices or is it bound by past practices? This was an issue in the last steel strike and was the issue in the railroad strike. Dr. Charles Killingsworth of Michigan State, in a paper presented to the president's commission investigating the railroad strike, pointed to the comparison between the mass-production industries, where management generally is free to assign people, and the railroads, where the right of management to assign and make changes is severely limited by the collective bargaining agreement.

This was an issue in the West Coast dock negotiations and is an issue on the East Coast where negotiations on the size of dock crews are taking place.

Yet, the essence of management's function is really the ability to adapt to change. Management really is managing change. The hallmark of our country is change, and management works to harness these forces of change.

To cite an example from the automobile industry: In 1958, Rambler had about one per cent of the business. But the market was changing. There was a recession that year—for everyone except Rambler. Currently Rambler accounts for five to six per cent of the business. Had American Motors not moved quickly, and not capitalized on the opportunity, it would be dead today.

What we **really** want to preserve in our country is the ability to adapt to change—using new techniques, meeting new situations. Therefore, management's basic function is to manage change. Frequently collective bargaining interferes with this function because change implies disruption of established relationships. This is really the basic issue involved in management's rights—what things can management do unilaterally and what things does it have to share with its employees?

Management Rights Under Labor Act

This is not an absolute right, nor is it one that is clearly defined in collective bargaining or otherwise. Those in the private industry labor-management relationship operate under the National Labor Relations Act. There is a clause in the Act that says the union shall represent employees in the determination of wages, hours, and other conditions of work. One of the pioneers in labor economics, George Taylor, pointed out that that little phrase, "other conditions of work," is an open-end phrase because there is no definition of what "other conditions" are.

Over the years, the law has tended to expand the subject matter that is to be included in collective bargaining and decisions have been handed down on the inclusion of pensions, insurance, etc., as legitimate subjects. Currently, some of the decisions of the National Labor Relations Board have held that many rights which management thought were its own, unilaterally, were not. Sub-contracting is an example of such a decision.

25

Changing Role of Arbitrator

The court's view of the changing role of the arbitrator has had a dramatic impact. Most contracts in the auto industry—and quite generally elsewhere—provide for a private arbitrator who rules on disputes between the parties within the framework of the contract. He does not help them negotiate a new contract, but he makes decisions interpreting the existing contract.

The Supreme Court, in a series of three decisions called the "Warrior Trilogy," gave the arbitrator a tremendous amount of power and latitude, at least in management's view. The court said the arbitrator's awards were not subject to court review unless they were clearly beyond his authority. In fact, this gave the arbitrator the right to decide whether a subject raised by either party was subject to the arbitration clause. In other words, the arbitrator could decide how far his own authority should reach. As a result, General Electric's arbitration clause, which used to be a few paragraphs, is now several pages long.

Basic Obligations Evolving

Many companies are concerned about limiting the arbitrator's right under this kind of an open-ended authority. These, of course, are legal questions. The bread-and-butter of this subject involves the union-management relationship; it is here the basic obligations are decided with respect to employees and management.

There are two schools of thought here. One is not to spell out all management rights, because some might be left out. Instead, all rights not specifically granted to the union are reserved for management. Sometimes the arbitrator and the courts will uphold this and sometimes they will not.

There is another school of thought that thinks all management rights should be listed because if any are omitted, somebody will say they do not belong to management. Probably most contracts try to take a middle road by saying that if any rights have been omitted, they still belong to management.

Profit Sharing in a Union Shop

American Motors Corporation's management rights clause epitomizes the whole problem. In 1961, this organization negotiated a profit sharing plan with the UAW, and subsequently with other unions. There was considerable discussion among other companies that the profit-sharing contract would automatically involve the union in many areas of management's rights. In other words, by involving the

26

union in the profit-sharing part of wages, it might then have the right to question management's judgment on product, pricing, advertising, manufacturing schedules, and so on.

Most other profit-sharing plans exist either in non-union companies or are not subject to negotiation with the union. In any event, to try and overcome this problem or rather, to forestall any difficulties, the company negotiated a comprehensive management rights clause with the union. Interestingly enough, it was probably the first time that the UAW has agreed to a limitation on its own rights.

This clause is rather lengthy. As a matter of fact, it is not strictly a management rights clause—it is a rights of both-parties clause, because the union's rights are enumerated also.

The clause begins by saying: "The parties to the agreement recognize that they are engaged in a common endeavor in which each of them have separate and distinct responsibilities, which both of them are obligated to meet in a manner consistent with their mutual over-riding responsibility to the community as a whole." Then there is a pledge of cooperation and it goes on to say: "The union recognizes the right of management to maximum freedom to manage, consistent with due regard for the welfare and interests of the employees."

Specific rights belonging solely to management are identified, such as the determination of product, marketing, financing, organizing productive business, record keeping, etc. In another section it states that in the absence of the profit sharing plan, the union would have no more rights than it had in the past, in a normal collective bargaining relationship.

Management Rights Identified

The management group believes that management rights fall into four categories. First, those which are purely unilateral, and must not be delegated or assigned to non-management groups. They include pricing of the product, methods of accounting, plant location, manufacturing scheduling, assignment of employees, etc.

Second is a group of management rights that should be shared with employees, at least to the extent of communicating their actions to the organized group. Not to get their agreement, not for discussion, nor consultation, but only as a matter of communication, so that they know what will take place. In this area are such activities as notice of production schedules, viewing next year's product, and notice of changes in management personnel.

A third group of responsibilities are best discharged by listening to the employees' desires, without having to agree to a change. This is a kind of two-way communication. Discussions in this area cover such things as the option of scheduling two half-days, one before Christmas and one before New Year's, versus one full day on and one full day off. What the employees want is considered and if not incompatible with management's ideas, is then adopted.

Lastly, are those areas where responsibility must be shared.

The philosophy at AM is that collective bargaining as a national institution must be upgraded. The co-operative relationship must be improved. One of the ways to improve it, obviously, is for management to communicate with the employees, to give them a greater feeling of participation, and without giving away any management rights.

Union Relations in Public Sector

In the public sector, union relationships are in a greater state of ferment than in the private sector. Unions have not grown particularly over-all, but what growth has occurred, has been largely in the public area. In Detroit, for instance, a collective bargaining election for teachers was held and they selected the Detroit Federation of Teachers as their bargaining agent. A similar move was made in Cleveland.

It is not intended to suggest that there is an absolute parallel between management rights in the public area and management rights in the private sector of the economy. But obviously there is a common management function. Every organization has a management function including the unions. Recently, the field representatives of the UAW felt that they ought to have a union of their own to deal with the UAW and Walter Reuther.

Political vs. Administrative Authority

There are different circumstances in the public sector than in private management. For instance, the authority is different from the authority in private industry. A common thread runs through many of the articles appearing in the journals of public administration. This is the problem of political authority vs. the administrative authority and reconciling the two to find out who is management. Who has the responsibility ultimately? It's a chicken-and-egg matter—the people you are responsible for supervising are also voters who are responsible for the kind of administration they have.

The basic problem of management in any area is to provide competent leadership. In the public sector there are certain rights that cannot be shared; the sovereignty of the state is involved. On the other hand, there are some limitations on the employee's right to strike. In private collective bargaining, ultimately the right to strike is the final indicator of how strongly either side feels about the matters at issue. If there is no such mechanism, there is greater responsibility placed on management. It may be more d.fficult to hold on and administer management's rights than where the employee has recourse to a strike.

In our society, however, it is the people who ultimately determine the extent of management's rights. There are very few absolutes, and basically it is the way in which management rights are exercised that determines whether the people will support discharging the legitimate function of management. This support does not depend on whether employees are unionized or not. If employees think management is acting in a fair, responsible manner, the question of whether these actions are unilateral is not important. Rights imply responsibilities. It is more important that employees believe management is discharging its responsibility fairly and equitably, and that they are being heard.

Precedent Influences Decision

Finally, the best management rights clause in the world is no good if it is not exercised. In collective bargaining in private industry, a major problem is not the contract language, but the day-to-day administration of the personnel program. Much can be lost because the supervisors do not understand what their responsibilities are—what their rights are—and either give away rights that were fought hard for, or they do not exercise them. When a crisis comes it is usually discovered that management does not possess the rights it thought it did.

Arbitrators put a great deal of emphasis on past practice. Even though a right exists on paper, if it has been consistently ignored its effectiveness may be lost. There is no substitute for sound personnel policies for developing a sense of fairness and equity among employees, whether unionized or not. Ultimately, a right can only be retained to the extent to which it is discharged fairly and equitably.

4. Development of Written Employee Relations Policies

Theodore H. Lang

As a practitioner in the public personnel field for the past 25 years, I have been involved both in the development of written employee relations policies and in their maintenance and enforcement. And I have had the opportunity to view these processes from several vantage points—as a central personnel agency technician, as an operating agency personnel officer, as a central personnel agency official, as a member of the faculty of New York University's School of Public Administration, and now as the New York City Personnel Director. Yet I must admit that the need to think the subject through and prepare this paper, has probably done more to crystallize my thinking than all the years of practice.

Formulation of Policy

Many of the people who look on government procedures as "bureaucratic red tape" have charged that formalized employee relations policies have serious limitations. They say the decisions the policies compel lack common sense and bind the administrator.

Provide Equitable Employee Treatment

Cases can of course be cited where personnel rules were ineffective, or even worse, hampered action to the detriment of the organization. It would seem as though these critics believe the administrator can operate best in maximum freedom. This is nonsense. Just as soon as the administrator is freed, he, himself, finds it necessary to develop his own policies to guide his decisions and conduct.

A large organization cannot operate efficiently without formalized employee relations policies. Such policies are essential for equity of treatment of employees throughout the organization. They are essential for a reasonable degree of continuity in the organization from year to year. They will generally avoid much more trouble than they cause if they are intelligently developed. They can promote efficient operation so that decisions can be made promptly on personnel matters without profound consideration of each item of business. The personnel business of the organization could not be done well without personnel policies. In a sense, they contribute to the "ingrained habit" of the organization which enables the organization to conduct a large part of its business efficiently and economically and to devote time to major new problems.

I cite merely one illustration, namely policies for dealing with the problem of employees who are physically or mentally incapable of satisfactory performance. Great sensitivity is needed to protect the interests of the employee and of the public. Several alternative courses of action are possible depending upon age and service of the employee, diagnosis and prognosis of the employee's illness, and nature of the job he fills. A well considered, fully explored policy is essential. This cannot be done by each unit of government each time a case arises. Existence of such an established policy is a guide and a relief for the administrator.

Involve All Interested Parties

No personnel policy can be formulated in a vacuum; all must be prepared within a framework that includes the constitution or charter and the laws of the jurisdiction and the mores and traditions of the jurisdiction. Although the laws and culture of a community guide and control policy formulation, neither are immutable. It is within the function of the policy-maker to seek the changes he believes are needed. That these efforts must generally be approached with great care and planning and a broad educational campaign is evident.

In the formulation of employee relations policies, it is important to follow procedures that will help disclose serious mistakes before a policy is announced. It can be extremely damaging to management when avoidable errors have to be corrected. We Met fans in New York City call this defensive action "touching bases." Thus, there should be communication with employees and unions concerning major personnel policies under consideration and an opportunity to protest and present different points of view. The same is true for line officials. As a matter of preference, I would recommend that the clearances with government officials be made first, before the proposed personnel policy is sent to employees and employee groups.

It is even desirable to go beyond "touching bases" and involve personnel people throughout the organization in the development of personnel policies on a problem-oriented basis. One way to accomplish this type of involvement is through a personnel council or an agency cabinet. Policies developed through such organs tend to be more effective; have fewer "bugs"; and, most importantly, are implemented and supported by the decision-makers up and down the line.

The technique of communication among all interested parties is frequently more important to successful development of policies than is the substance of the policy. I have seen excellent policies arouse controversy because they were not "cleared." Both the union leader and the government administrator are apt to react negatively if a new policy is sprung on them without warning, and they will look for a weakness in the new item which can be attacked. To avoid attack, to avoid serious error, to avoid embarrassing "bugs," to avoid need for sudden withdrawal or amendment of a new policy, "touch bases."

Of course, with every rule there is an exception and there may be times when it is advisable not to touch bases, but there is always a calculated risk in skipping this step.

Build In Flexibility

Much of the charge that personnel operations are rigid can be avoided by providing for some choice of decision on the part of the supervisor, making employee benefits permissive rather than mandatory, allowing a common-sense flexibility before a decision is made on an employee. For example, the techniques of consultation discussed above will tend to promote flexibility. Below are illustrations of "built-in flexibility," cited from New York City's policies. The discretionary clause or phrase has been underlined for purposes of this presentation:

Pay Plan Regulation

5.2 In the case of any issue or cause for interpretation arising in connection with the provisions of the Career and Salary Plan Resolution or the provisions of these regulations the Director of the Budget and the Personnel Director shall be jointly empowered to make pro tempore rulings in connection therewith subject to submission to the Board of Estimate within 60 days for final approval and inclusion in these regulations by the Board of Estimate.

Leave Regulations

2.8 Penalties for unexcused tardiness may be imposed by the head of each agency in conformance with established rules of the agency. As a minimum, however, all unexcused tardiness both in the morning and upon return from lunch shall be charged to the annual leave allowance.

2.9 Terminal leave with pay upon retirement may be allowed in the discretion of the agency head not to exceed one month for every ten years of service, pro-rated for a fractional part thereof. The agency head shall be guided in this matter by the character of service rendered and by the manner and extent of use of sick leave credits by the employee.

32

3.2 Sick leave <u>may</u> be granted <u>in the discretion of the agency
head</u> and proof of disability must be provided by the employee, <u>satisfactory to the agency head</u>. Presentation of a
physician's certificate in the prescribed form may be
waived for absences up to and including three consecutive
work days. In a case of a protracted disability, such certificate shall be presented to the agency head at the end of
each month of continued absence.

Service Rating Regulations

4.1 The City Civil Service Commission: (a) may, subject to
its review and approval, <u>authorize an agency to establish
its own performance rating program</u>; (b) shall consider
and determine appeals from employees and may modify
agency ratings; and (c) may audit such programs. The
Commission may at any time revoke its authorization to
an agency to establish and maintain its own evaluation program.

4.2 The Department of Personnel shall: (a) investigate and
report to the Commission on performance rating appeals;
(b) review and report to the Commission on the operation
of agency performance rating programs; and (c) <u>provide
consulting service to agencies requesting assistance in developing and maintaining performance rating programs</u>.

4.3 <u>Each agency operating its own performance rating program</u>
shall submit to the Department of Personnel a statement of
the performance ratings assigned to its employees and
shall maintain appropriate records in its own offices of the
performance and ratings of the individual employees.

Strengthen Supervisory Decision-Making

Policies like those just quoted will tend to strengthen supervisory decision-making and decentralization of authority. Both are
especially important in large organizations that are spread over
wide geographic areas. The City of New York has a central set of
rules and regulations on leave practices that apply to approximately 150,000 employees, yet the individual agency head can promul-
gate his own set of rules, which may amplify or supplement, but
cannot be in conflict with the central set of rules.

Choose Proper Legal Instrument

Another question to be considered when formulating personnel
policies is: Into which legal instruments should they be incorporated? They may be: legislation, executive orders, civil service rules,

agency rules, and administrative orders. A given policy can be incorporated in any one of these instruments, and part of the task of developing employee relations policies is the determination of the instrument to carry the policy. In making this decision, one must consider the values and defects of each of these instruments.

Legislation. I have a firm conviction that except for major policies of the broadest type and those involving major financial commitments such as pension systems, it is not wise to fix personnel policies in legislation. If done, a major defect—so far as the administrator is concerned—is that the courts become involved in administrative matters and often make decisions that can hamstring administration. Also, the difficulty of changing laws and the time consumed in making such changes hamper administrative adjustment to current situations and problems. Another weakness is that the legislature usually does not have expertise in very technical areas and prefers to fix broad public policy and to delegate a quasi-legislative power to an administrative body to fill in the details. Finally, the matter becomes too involved in policies, and pressures rather than merit will determine the final outcome. The effectiveness of pressure tactics on legislators is illustrated by a trend for employee groups to seek legislation that will provide a high degree of protection to the employee on discipline and on reserve promotional opportunities to the "in-group" by barring lateral entry into the service.

Quasi-legislative instruments. For most employee relations policies, executive orders, civil service rules, agency rules, and administrative orders are to be preferred over legislation. Executive orders and civil service rules have a jurisdiction-wide impact as do laws, yet they have the value of being more amenable to administrative change and interpretation and can better be decided on the merits of promoting good management.

Among the employee relations areas which are covered by executive orders in New York City are the pay plan, the time and leave regulations, grievance procedures, and collective bargaining. Among those which are covered by civil service rules are the classification plan, rules on probationary period, rules on transfers, reinstatements, and discipline. All of these could have been incorporated in legislation, but it was felt that to do so would deprive the city of flexibility.

Agency rules are essential, and within the agency, administrative orders have an important role in the fixing of procedures. As we have seen, agency rules permit fine adjustment to specific program needs, area needs, and special problems and missions of agencies.

Subjects Covered in Formal Personnel
Policy Statements

A full discussion of the subjects to be covered in formal personnel policy statements would fill a book. They are, therefore, only listed below. In most cases, the mere listing is self-explanatory and is adequate as an inventory of this subject. The instrument in which the policy appears in New York City is indicated parenthetically, with abbreviations having the following meanings: Civil Service Rules (CSR); Executive Order (EO); Administrative Order (AO); Law (L); Agency Rules (AR).

A. The classification plan and its administration (CSR)

B. 1. The pay plan and its administration, including pay scales, allocations of classes to pay grades and pay plan allocations (EO)
   2. Fringe benefits
   3. Pension and retirement

C. Time and leave regulations (EO)

D. Grievance procedures (EO)

E. Union relations including dues check-off and collective bargaining (EO)

This is a most sensitive area requiring careful preplanning. Policy changes made in this area are difficult to reverse. The menace of the strike and the strike threat must be kept in mind, and these policies should be so designed as to militate against strikes and strike threats from the outset.

F. Training and other employee development programs

G. Incentives policy

   1. Service awards (EO)
   2. Merit awards (EO and AO)
   3. Merit salary increases (EO)
   4. Suggestion program

H. Employe conduct

   1. On-the-job (AR and L)
   2. Restrictions on political activity (L)
   3. Code of ethical conduct (L)
   4. Moonlighting and dual job employment (AR and CSR)
   5. Nepotism (AR)
   6. Off-the-job conduct (AR)

I. Evaluation

    1. Probationary period (CSR and AR)
    2. Performance evaluation (L, CSR, and AR)

J. Employe health

    1. Health, hospital plans and blood banks (L, EO, and AR)
    2. Safety program (L)
    3. Injury incurred in course of employment, including workmen's compensation (L, EO, and AR)
    4. Disabled employee—physical and mental disability (AR)
    5. Optional annual examination (AR and EO)
    6. Mandated medical examinations (AR and EO)

K. Promotion policy

L. Reduction-in-force policy—Lay-offs (L and CSR)

M. Transfers, reinstatements, and assignments policy (CSR)

N. Discipline—standards, charges, notice, hearing, counsel penalties and appeals (L, CSR, and AR)

O. Official investigations

    1. Requirement to testify (L)
    2. Requirement to notify agency (EO and AR)
    3. Resignations under fire (EO and AR)

Subjects Omitted from Formal Personnel Policy Statements

It may be inadvisable to put some personnel policies into writing because formal action might destroy the usefulness of the policy. Instead, questions that arise may be handled temporarily as special orders or special administrative decisions, in the hope that the pressures causing the problems can eventually be eliminated.

As an illustration of this situation, it is the policy of New York City not to grant time for religious observance, but to allow an adequate amount of annual leave time for each employee to satisfy his religious obligations. Despite this opportunity and generous leave allowance—ranging from 20 to 27 workdays a year—there are insistent pressures annually to make special grants of time on special religious holy days. This has been resisted with minor exceptions. These exceptions, although regularly made, are not incorporated in the formal leave policy of the City. There are other occasions when a special privilege may be granted to employees in a given year.

With the onset of collective bargaining, it may be the better part of wisdom not to fix such privileges in the written policy of the jurisdiction, but rather to hold back a formal policy for bargaining purposes. It is not always possible to be completely frank on all policy matters and on all directions of policy change.

Dissemination and Maintenance of Personnel Policies

It is important to employ the proper methods for development of policy and the proper instrument in which to incorporate the policy. But if the policy is to be fully effective, observed, and supported, a system must be established for dissemination and maintenance of personnel policies. This was brought to my attention dramatically only a few weeks ago. I had preferred charges against an employee who had failed to comply with agency rules relating to the reporting of the fact that a relative of the employee was taking a civil service examination. The hearing officer whom I appointed to hear the charges recommended that the employee be found not guilty, because there was an inadequate record of his having received the agency rules and no indication of his having had an opportunity to study them. Therefore, if employees are to be held responsible for agency rules, especially rules concerning employee conduct both on and off the job, it is important that the rules be disseminated to the employees, and, preferably, a record be made that the employee has received and studied the rules.

Media for Communicating Policy

It is important that there be adequate communication of policies to employees, supervisors, executives, and personnel managers and technicians. Personnel policies can be incorporated in the following instruments for employees:

1. Agency rules for employees
2. Employee handbooks
3. Staff orders which are circulated and initialed
4. Booklet on leave regulations
5. Suggestion program manual
6. Code of ethics and decisions of the board of ethics

For supervisors, the following instruments should be helpful:

1. Central personnel agency rules and regulations
2. Booklet on employee relation programs
3. Separate guides for supervisors in such fields as: employee grievances, probationary period, discipline and performance evaluations

In addition to the above, it is useful to have available for executives and personnel officers bound looseleaf compilations of laws and rules, and interpretations thereof.

Keep Policy Current

Personnel policy won't stay "fixed." Conditions change, work programs change, equipment changes, laws change, problems change, and it is essential that policies also change to meet all new conditions. As changes are made in policies, it is important that there be a regular procedure for maintaining a printed document so that changes will be sent to interested parties. Responsibility must be placed on one unit or one individual for maintaining the instrument in which the policies are defined. As a matter of regular procedure, I recommend strongly that any rule book which is printed and bound and made available to employees be reprinted periodically—perhaps every two or three years—so that copies are available for both new and old employees, and management is sure that the copy in the hands of the employee is not significantly outdated. Some sort of looseleaf treatment, with periodic transmittal of new pages—perhaps every three months—is probably best for those officials who must have accurate, up-to-the-minute personnel policy information.

In my judgment, the procedure for maintaining the policy instrument should itself be defined in writing, probably in a set of administrative orders of the agency, and audit techniques should be set up to insure compliance with policies. There can be audit of time records, payroll records, leave of absence applications and forms, classification decisions, agency examinations, etc. Audit is essential to insure compliance with policies, just as policing is essential to insure compliance with law. Policies that are not enforced soon become ignored. This is a truism of human beings and society. Audit or review of policy implementation need not be an expensive proposition. It should not be done on a 100 per cent basis; it can be done on a sampling basis. The sampling itself need not be of a size to insure scientific reliability although this would be desirable. The mere existence of an audit of any kind serves to "jack up" the organization and leads to major compliance with policies.

Periodic Review of Personnel Policy System

Personnel policy must be kept alive and current. Usually this takes place on a problem basis rather than on an over-all review basis, and this is perfectly satisfactory. As I come to the end of this review of the development of written employee relations policies, it seems evident to me that a periodic review of the entire personnel policy system is valuable for the purpose of determining if all important areas have been covered adequately. But it is also desirable for any organization to look on a broad, over-all basis at its personnel policies and the manner in which they are handled to determine whether or not any repair or drastic overhaul is necessary.

Conclusion

In the review of a personnel policy system, there are a number of tests that can be applied which can be a helpful guide to the soundness of the system.

Test of Comprehensiveness

Does the policy system cover all of the areas that need to be covered? Are the instruments being used for policy performance adequate and maintained properly? Are the policies effective?

Test of Flexibility

Does the policy system lead to decisions which, when tested on their own merits, are unwise? Does it force an administrator to make an unsound decision because the policy mandates an action he does not want to take? Is decision-making left to the supervisor in authority? Can the rules and policies meet the needs of all the agencies in all the geographical areas in which they are to be applied?

Test of Continuity

Do the supervisors and the employees have a sense of a well-managed organization with security from erratic changes in policy which zig-zag from the extremely strict to the lenient? Can a supervisor rely upon standards with which he has become familiar? Likewise, can an employee develop knowledge of what is expected and behave accordingly, without finding that standards have changed drastically without adequate notification?

Test of Placement of Authority and Responsibility

It is an axiom in the field of management that if anyone is to be held responsible for a given operation, he must have the authority to make the decisions needed to conduct the operation. Rules which divide authority and responsibility are bad. If a supervisor is to be held responsible for performance of subordinates, he must have adequate authority in respect to compensation, probationary period, discipline, etc.

Test of Cost

It is possible to regulate too much, to specify too much, to bind too much activity by rule. Any system of management must be tested by its cost. Many personnel policies have a major financial impact, e.g., collective bargaining, pension, and leave allowances. Managers must manage within the funds available. Liberal pensions, leave regulations, fringe benefits are extremely costly in today's society, amounting to a substantial percentage of the regular salary of an employee—as much as from 30 to 50 per cent. The ultimate squeeze is on the elected leader who must seek taxes. Cost must always be kept in mind in fixing any personnel relations policy. This is the reason why budget people are always closely involved in personnel matters—not always to the delight of the personnel man.

Test of Promoting the Mission of the Organization

After all, the organization does not exist so that personnel men can have jobs or so that employees can have vacations and pensions and rights and privileges. Above all else, there is the purpose for which the organization was established—the so-called mission of the organization. Policies must contribute to the mission of the organization. This must be kept in mind at all times, and therefore it is important that line officials with basic responsibility for the mission of the organization be involved in any policy formulation.

5.

Before Collective Bargaining Begins

Lew Fay

One of these days—sooner than some of us are willing to believe—we will have collective bargaining in all, or most, public agencies. Many of us are already faced with the fact. The size of this group, however, is minute compared to the number of agencies which have little or no formal dealings with employee associations. There are those who do not discuss any of the topics usually covered by collective bargaining agreements with employee representatives. In some agencies, there is a distinct aversion to unions and to anything but the most docile type of employee organization. This attitude can only lead to trouble.

In recent years, the tide of collective bargaining in public employment has swept across those parts of the United States where organized labor has substantial power. The froth of this tidal wave has spread into areas which previously have been deserts in the landscape of industrial democracy. There is every evidence that collective bargaining in the public service is not too far off for many of us. Shall we just wait until it hits us? Or is there something we should be doing about it?

I believe there is a most important middle step for those of us who have not yet been confronted with collective bargaining. There are two fundamental components to this middle step: good will and good communications.

Prime Element Is Good Will

Good will is the most important element. It can create the climate of mutual willingness to get along and to negotiate in good faith. Obviously, good communications without good will can produce nothing but imprecations.

Good will, then, is a basic ingredient of the middle step. Management at all levels and personnel people must understand that collective bargaining cannot be overtly despised. Even if there is prejudice against unions, it must not be revealed, and a sincere effort must be made to eradicate it.

Employers get exactly the kind of employee relations they deserve. Tough bosses create tough unions. Regardless of occasional disenchantments, it is still fundamentally true that people react in a good way to good treatment.

Most of us probably would agree that the "inner-man" needs of the employer and the employee are very much the same: both want security, dignity, appreciation, recognition, accomplishment. This agreement is not found so frequently, however, when external goals and desires, like making money and gaining power, are considered. The desires are alike, but the targets are often separated because of a lack of mutual understanding and respect.

Interdependence Stressed

Employer-employee relationships, which lack good will, usually are the result of an instinctive belief on the part of the employer that agency objectives can be realized without regard to the objectives of employees—and vice versa. The only way that the two targets can be brought closer together is for both the employer and the employee to realize that each is dependent upon the other.

In recent years, California state assemblymen have proposed several bills aimed toward making collective bargaining and binding arbitration a requirement for all public agencies in the state. The preoccupation of several of the state legislators in California with collective bargaining has increased rapidly during the last six years. So far none of these proposals has passed, except for some rather mild (and much needed) regulations giving all public employees the right to organize and be represented.

Because of the obvious direction and, I believe, ultimate success of this political trend, in 1959, I decided to form a labor-management advisory group. The purpose was to get used to talking among ourselves without self-consciousness or suspicion. After a deliberately long exploratory and expository period, during which I planted the idea with my various bosses and others—my civil service commissioners, the city councilmen, the city manager, the union and unaffiliated employee group leaders, department heads, and so on—we had the first of our monthly meetings on October 30, 1960.

Personnel Advisory Council

We called this group the Personnel Advisory Council (advisory to me). In our first minutes the tone and the tenor of the organization was recorded: the Personnel Advisory Council would be an unofficial but influential labor-management committee. Objectives of the committee would be:

1. Improve two-way communications in the agency.

2. Provide a forum for the exchange of ideas.

3. Foster the collaborative development of personnel policy proposals.

4. Advise the personnel director on all personnel matters.

In the three years of its existence, the Personnel Advisory Council has been extremely productive and helpful. Let me tell you why I think it has worked out so well:

1. The membership of my Personnel Advisory Council is balanced. Management and employee groups are represented equally. In our agency, we have managerial and nonmanagerial (independent) departments. Managerial members are the senior assistant to the city manager and one of the major department heads under the manager's jurisdiction who has frequent dealings with employee groups, such as the public works director. Departments which are not under the manager are represented by two "independent" directors or their assistants. One of these is a chief deputy city attorney, who gives us legal advice as well as his opinions on the policies under consideration. Four employee groups are represented. Two are internationally affiliated unions and two are local, unattached associations.

2. We have one or more alternates for each regular member. Thus, we always have perfect attendance. An added benefit of having alternates is that it allows many more people to become active in the policy-making processes. This, in turn, helps "sell" the Personnel Advisory Council and the ideas which generate from the group.

3. All department and division heads are invited to work through the regular or alternate members who they know personally if they want to express an opinion on any present or needed personnel policy or procedure.

4. Personnel Advisory Council news is printed in, and given extended distribution by the city manager's Weekly Bulletin and by the publications of employee groups.

5. Meetings are completely informal, except for the publication of minutes. These minutes are based on stenographic notes taken of each discussion and usually are written as identified, indirect quotations with any necessary explanatory facts interwoven in the narrative. We deliberately avoid "lining up," with employees on one side of the conference table and managers on the other. We do not vote, but we record any final opinion which is different from the general consensus of the group. Rarely is there any dissension after a subject has been thoroughly explored.

6. We never rush or press for a decision. If an item proves to

43

be controversial when it is introduced, we sometimes keep the topic on the agenda for as long as three or four months.

7. Personnel Advisory Council minutes are distributed to all regular and alternate members, to the mayor and councilmen, to all department heads, and to the civil service commissioners. This wide distribution has greatly increased our readers' interest in the project, has rewarded employee and management representatives with proper personal recognition and publicity of their views, and has prepared the way for passage of the policy proposals which we develop collaboratively in the Personnel Advisory Council.

8. One of the more important reasons for the success of the Personnel Advisory Council is the fact that the City of San Diego is fortunate in having good, sensible, responsible employee representatives. It is worth repeating here that we would not have this ideal type of employee representation if we had not had a history of mutual good will.

Achievements Are Noteworthy

The Personnel Advisory Council's accomplishments in just three years have been numerous as well as noteworthy. Major projects so far have been concerned with the introduction of departmental Improvement Committees (labor-management extensions of the Personnel Advisory Council), supervisory training in employee performance ratings, extension of our original probationary period from six months to one year, modification of formal disciplinary procedures, and broadening the promotional opportunities of employees. An outstanding accomplishment of the Council was the establishment and development of a suggestion awards program which had been repeatedly turned down by previous managers and councilmen.

Other important developments resulted in an agency-wide code of ethics, ideas for better manpower utilization, and clarification of civil service rules. Currently we are discussing a payroll bank deposit plan. If adopted, there would be a great savings of manpower now spent in preparing and delivering individual payroll checks. Under this plan, employee earnings would be sent directly to one or more banks in which employees automatically would have checking accounts.

As satisfying as the tangible results of the Personnel Advisory Council's activities have been, one of the most gratifying aspects of the Council's meetings has been the frequency with which employees and management find they are in agreement. The middle step has brought us success and hope for the future.

6.

Techniques of Negotiation

Paul M. Berthoud

Scope of Collective Bargaining

Professional personnel administrators introduced to the mysteries of collective bargaining for the first time will quickly see that "collective bargaining" is used in two different senses. In a narrow sense, collective bargaining is the process by which an employer and a union that represents his employees negotiate an agreement covering the rates of pay, rules, and working conditions of the employees in the collective bargaining unit. In a broader sense, however, collective bargaining is the union-management relationship that arises as a consequence of a union being recognized as the representative of the employees. It includes the day-to-day discussion of grievances, management actions affecting employees, and other matters, as well as the narrower area of contract negotiations.

This paper deals only with collective bargaining in its limited sense—the negotiation of a contract for the first time after the union is recognized as representing the employees, or the negotiation of a new contract to replace a previously existing one. Throughout, however, it should be kept in mind that collective bargaining in the broad concept always influences the contract negotiation process. Contract negotiations are only a small part of the total collective bargaining relationship. What is done on a daily basis to solve employee relations problems and how management handles the employee relations aspects of management decisions determines, in great measure, what the contract negotiations will be like. For example, in some companies employee dissatisfaction may be so great that more time is spent in negotiations rehashing past incidents that the union or the employees think were not handled properly than discussing future wages and fringe benefits.

Management Objectives in Negotiations

Management has four basic goals in any contract negotiation. Each goal, however, has a number of facets, and they all must be considered if management is able to achieve a "balanced" agreement concerning pay, rules, and working conditions.

Preserve and Strengthen the Business

Management's first concern is to preserve and strengthen the business. One objective of this goal is to arrive at a settlement that will cost an amount the enterprise believes it can bear. Another objective is to maintain a competitive position in terms of labor expense. Today, almost every business competes with other businesses, either with the same product or with alternative products. To compete pricewise, a business cannot pay labor costs much higher than the costs of its competitors who produce the same product; neither can it pay labor costs that will raise the price of the product to the point where the consumer will turn to alternative products.

In my industry—the airline industry—the price of the product is approved by a regulatory agency and is normally uniform for all air carriers supplying the same service. Since labor costs represent such a large proportion of every expense dollar—roughly 42¢ —there is a strong incentive for each airline to be competitive with the other airlines in terms of labor costs.

Still another objective of management is avoidance of a strike. Any interruption in the operation of the business will certainly not strengthen that business.

Retain Control of the Business

The second management goal in negotiations—to retain control of the business—includes the avoidance of unreasonable restrictions on management's ability to manage the business in an efficient and economical manner.

There is a theory of labor relations called "the management's residual rights" theory. It begins with the premise that in the absence of a union or any other type of employee representation management has all rights. The collective bargaining contract represents those rights that management gives up. Management retains, as residual rights, all those rights not specifically limited by the collective bargaining contract. According to the residual rights theory, then, any collective bargaining contract is a restriction on management's right to manage the business. In practice, however, the question is not: Should there be restrictions? The question is: Are the restrictions reasonable?

In this day and age, for example, everyone would undoubtedly agree that it would be unreasonable for management to expect to work employees twelve hours a day, seven days a week. However, management's aim in negotiations will be to set hours of work that it believes will help, not handicap, the company's ability to operate

46

as efficiently and economically as possible. In negotiations, management will also try to eliminate restrictions such as "featherbedding"—the creation or retention of unneeded jobs. One example of featherbedding from the field of airline labor relations has been the problem of the flight engineer on the jet aircraft. Some airlines agreed with the Pilots' Association to man the jets with a pilot-qualified flight engineer and, additionally, agreed with the Flight Engineers' Union to man the jet with a flight engineer who did not have pilot qualifications. Only one flight engineer was needed operationally. The carriers agreed to the unnecessary man because of pressure from the two competing unions, and they have been trying to work their way out of that agreement ever since. In fact, an Emergency Board, appointed by the President to investigate a dispute on one of the carriers involved, said that the agreement was an error of collective bargaining; the carrier should not have agreed to put into the cockpit an employee who was not needed. It certainly is essential to management's retaining control of the business to keep the right to determine how many employees are needed to do the work.

Buttress Over-all Personnel Policy

The third management goal in negotiations is to arrive at a settlement that will help to implement the enterprise's over-all personnel policies. It is every employer's personnel policy to create and maintain a contented and productive work force that is directed toward achieving the goals of the enterprise. The negotiation and the settlement that result should be considered in the light of this over-all personnel policy.

In some situations, for example, because of economic strength, the employer can force an inexpensive settlement or settle for less than the terms that are justifiable on the basis of the objective facts. When an employer drives such a bargain, he runs the risk of sabotaging his own personnel policy. In other words, a settlement that is "too good" from the employer's standpoint may cause morale problems. It may also cause internal union problems if the employees become dissatisfied with their representatives. The long-term result may be extremely harmful from the employer's standpoint.

Establish Good Management-Union Relations

The fourth goal of management in negotiations is to establish a stable and businesslike relationship with the union representatives. This aspect of negotiations relates to the broad concept of collective bargaining. Management's relationship with its employee representatives does not begin at the start of negotiations and end with

the settlement. It continues through the contract term. To the full-
est extent possible, the contract negotiations should be used as a
foundation for a continued good working relationship. The discussion of mutual problems, usually for about four hours a day, gives
the employer the opportunity to know the union representative and
gives the union representative an opportunity to learn about the employer's attitude toward employee problems.

Union Objectives in Negotiations

The union also has certain main goals in every contract negotiation, and they, too, must be considered if management is to obtain a "balanced" agreement.

Preserve and Strengthen the Union

In my opinion, the first union objective in any negotiation is the
same as that of management—to preserve and strengthen the union
as an institution. I believe that union officers will agree that this
objective is usually considered even more important than the welfare of certain individual members. Let me give an illustration to
support this belief.

In some cases the union has as an over-all goal—the establishment of a uniform wage rate for a particular type of work. The union feels that the uniform rate sets a pattern, provides the greatest
benefit for the greatest percentage of the membership, and lays a
floor for future contract negotiations. Once such a pattern is set,
the union may be willing to strike—even though the striking employees will suffer financial hardship—in order to avoid breaking the
wage pattern and settling for a figure less than they feel is the going rate. Strike benefits, of course, never fully make up the financial loss to the striking employee.

Demonstrate the Union's Value

The union's second objective in negotiations is to get more for
its membership and thereby demonstrate to the members the union's value to them. Obviously, it is critically important from a union standpoint that the employees believe that they receive more as
a result of having a union represent them than they would if there
were no union looking after their interests. This belief is the union's lifeblood.

Gain More Control Over Jobs

The third union goal is greater control of jobs. This goal may be expressed in proposals to upgrade certain work for which a premium rate is paid. It may also be expressed in proposals to create more jobs to accomplish the same amount of work.

A proposal for the maintenance of complement is an example. If there are a specified number of jobs on a shift and an employee is absent for illness or other reasons, the union may seek a contract provision to require the filling of the absent employee's job on an overtime basis. For example, unions have exerted strong pressure on the airline industry to create "lead" jobs, jobs that are paid at a higher rate than the rate for the basic classification. Once created, there has been strong pressure to require the replacement of an absent lead by upgrading an employee from the basic classification. United Airlines contracts, for instance, now have a rule that says that when there are three or more employees on a shift and no supervisor is on duty, one employee will be a lead. This employee will lead and direct the other employees and be paid a premium rate of pay. Rules relating to crew size are an example of more jobs for the same amount of work.

Promote Social and Economic Goals

A fourth frequent union objective in negotiations is to promote broad social and economic goals. This union interest is reflected in strong support of pension plans, a benefit for an employee after he no longer works for the employer. Retraining in case of layoff and protection in case of displacement or layoff are other examples.

Promote Status of Representatives

In many cases, there is competition between unions or union representatives to increase the amount of settlement—just as there is competition between employers to hold down the cost of the negotiation. In other words, the interest of the employer is to arrive at a settlement that does not put him out of line costwise. The interest of the union representative is to maximize the amount of settlement and thereby advance his personal goals and ambitions. Should some other union representative negotiate a higher rate of pay in a comparable situation, he might well lose the support of his membership and his job.

Bargaining in Good Faith

Basic to the concept of collective bargaining is the legal obligation—on both the employer and the union—to bargain in good faith. This means simply that both parties must make a bona fide attempt to reach a settlement.

Bargaining in good faith does not require either the union or the employer to make any concessions. In other words, the employer can refuse to offer any wage increase because he feels his margin of profit inadequate or the wage rates he presently is paying are adequate. His position is not a violation of the duty to bargain in good faith so long as he has justifiable reasons for it.

One airline told the major unions with which it deals that it was on the verge of bankruptcy and, therefore, would not grant any wage increase. The airline maintained this position for several years in spite of heavy union pressure. Again, this was not a violation of the duty to bargain in good faith.

Similarly, the union has no obligation to retreat one inch from its original demands, inflated though the employer may think they are. In short, "good faith" means: The parties to the negotiation are obligated only to have reasonable grounds for their position.

The duty to bargain in good faith also requires the employer to produce, upon request, information necessary to the intelligent discussion of the negotiation issues. Information about the cost of proposals and the effect of the proposals upon the employer's operations are usually matters peculiarly within the knowledge of the employer. The employer, therefore, has the obligation to furnish this information so that the negotiations can be conducted on the basis of known facts.

How to Bargain

From the employer's standpoint, preparations for negotiations should be as thorough as it is possible to make them. He should keep in mind that the whole purpose of negotiations is to persuade the other party to agreement. In large measure, preparation supplies the stuff of persuasion.

Six tested techniques for contract negotiations preparation are discussed below:

1. Review grievance decisions since the last contract settlement to determine whether there are problem areas in terms of contract language or matters that should be covered by the contract which are not.

2. Get industry comparisons on wages and fringe benefits. The employer should have detailed information as to what his competitors are paying for like work and what his competitors' fringe benefit programs are. This information is essential for determining whether the result of the negotiation will keep the employer competitive. In my own organization, United Air

Lines, we also obtain data that enable us to compare our wage settlements and fringe benefit programs with industries outside of the airline industry. We analyze automobile manufacturing settlements, steel settlements, etc., because these settlements tend to set a national pattern. We make comparisons of what we have done with other groups of our own employees, including nonorganized employees. We try to maintain some equality of treatment between our organized and our nonorganized employees.

3. Determine the range of settlements in industry, generally. This range is usually expressed in terms of cents per hour. The Commerce Clearing House or the Bureau of National Affairs labor services provides this information on a monthly basis. The study will show what percentage of settlements falls within certain cents per hour ranges. Contract settlement statistics are wonderfully imprecise. Information is readily available in detailed form on the amounts of increase, but information on the duration of the contracts represented in the settlement figures is very sketchy. Obviously, the amount of the settlement is directly related to the duration of the contract. Additionally, the survey will not usually show the skill composition of the groups covered by the settlements. The survey, therefore, has value only if one can assume that the group of employees to be compared have an over-all skill level that is roughly equivalent to the nation's work force as a whole. The best advice is: Use fully all the information available.

4. Ask the departments affected by the forthcoming contract negotiations for comments and suggestions for management proposals to be put in the opening letter to the union. Try to involve first-level supervisors in the determination of these proposals. First-level supervisors have primary responsibility for administering the terms of a contract and presumably should have a good idea of the changes needed in the contract to help them do a better job. Try to have management's proposals represent a total management effort.

5. Prepare studies to illustrate and support management's proposals in the negotiations. In some cases, charts and graphs will help to illustrate a point. (For example, in a recent negotiation United proposed to take duties from several job classifications and assign them to another job classification. The employees who would do the additional duties under this proposal were ramp servicemen whose work was determined by the arrival and departure of flights. When there are no aircraft to take baggage and supplies to, they have a valley in their work. United wanted to fill in those valleys by taking work from other

classifications to level off the ramp serviceman's work load. This type of problem lent itself very well to a graphic presentation to the union negotiating committee. Unfortunately, the committee remained unpersuaded.)

6. Review the forthcoming negotiations with top management. Usually, thorough preparation before negotiations start will provide an approximation of what will be needed to reach a settlement. A top management review of his conclusions will assist the negotiator in two ways. First, he will normally have the assurance of management support of his position during the negotiation. Second, top management approval of the area of ultimate settlement allows the negotiator to aim his negotiating strategy toward a definite target. The negotiator and top management should realize, however, that the estimate is just that. Frequently, situations change during the course of the negotiation. Perhaps there is a new settlement with a major competitor that had not been reached at the time of the original review. The union may bring up an argument that had not been previously considered. In such cases, the negotiator may have to ask top management for additional authority.

Opening Proposals

The airlines and the railroads are covered by the Railway Labor Act. This law requires both the carrier and the union to serve notice of the specific changes desired in a collective bargaining agreement on the other party prior to the start of negotiations. The notice, in the case of the carrier, is simply a letter advising the union that, in accordance with Section 6 of the Railway Labor Act and the duration clause of the existing agreement, the carrier wishes to propose certain changes. The carrier then lists the changes and makes them specific enough so that the union knows what changes the carrier is trying to bring about, including the addition of new clauses. The carrier will at the same time get from the union a similar letter that will set forth what changes the union wants to make.

I believe the Railway Labor Act is the only statute regulating labor relations which requires that the parties exchange proposed changes prior to negotiations. It seems to me that this is a good way to begin negotiations and that it would be desirable to provide in the duration clause of every collective bargaining contract a provision that the union and management will exchange opening proposals prior to the start of negotiations. Some known benefits are these four:

1. The negotiators for both sides get some idea of the size of the problem before they go into negotiations. They do not find that the problem grows with every day of negotiations with

the introduction of new demands.

2. Both management and the union can make a careful analysis of the other side's proposals before being actually faced with them. It is possible, therefore, to do a little better job of preparing for negotiations and analyzing the problems. Anyone who has been in labor relations any length of time has gotten into a situation where, under time pressures, he agreed to something without knowing all of the facts and was sorry about it later. The better the proposal is analyzed, the more likely it is that such a situation will be avoided.

3. The exchange of opening proposals requires the union and management to crystallize their thinking on each of their proposals. (When United prepares an opening letter the nego- tiators meet with representatives of all of the operating depart- ments involved and try to work out company proposals that ev- eryone feels are justified. Frequently, ideas that seem a flash of intellectual lightning at the time turn out on careful review to be not such good ideas after all. The formality of preparing an opening proposal to be submitted in writing requires each party to think things through.)

4. The listing of the proposals provides a way of gauging the progress of the negotiations. When the number of propos- als is reduced, the negotiators realize they are getting down to the nub of the negotiations.

One thing to keep in mind is the effect on the employees of man- agement's proposals. If the company makes extreme opening pro- posals to gain bargaining room, the union can publicize the propos- als to the employees and whip up employee support for the union ne- gotiating committee. One airline put into its opening letter a pro- posal that rates of pay should be reduced in proportion to the less- ened productivity of the employees. The union distributed this pro- posal widely. The resulting employee reaction certainly did not make the subsequent negotiation any easier.

Location of Negotiations

Negotiation meetings are frequently held on "neutral" ground. The experience of United Air Lines has been that holding negotia- tions in its executive offices benefits both parties. This location makes available promptly company records that might be needed in the course of negotiations. Additionally, it makes available to the negotiating committees the service of experts in the company's headquarters on technical or complicated problems. For example, someone from the Insurance Department can quickly explain some aspect of the insurance program. United believes these are positive benefits that justify holding negotiations on company property. The unions have found also that meeting in the executive offices is desirable because they realize the easy availability of factual information serves to expedite the negotiations. Neutral ground is mutually inconvenient.

Negotiating Teams

It is standard practice for each side to have one spokesman. In some negotiations the union negotiating team is divided and does not present a unified view. When this occurs, agreement is impossible until the conflict is resolved. At United it is a personnel administration responsibility to provide the spokesman for the company's negotiating team. No one on the company's side of the table is authorized to agree to anything except the spokesman. The major operating departments of the company that are affected by the negotiations each have a representative on the team. They are there to offer advice to the spokesman and to provide knowledge of the day-to-day operation, but what the company is willing to do in relation to a particular proposal is a personnel administration responsibility.

There has been much discussion in labor relations circles about the authority of the negotiation committees to make binding commitments with no restriction as to authority. Accordingly, the question arises whether the company spokesman should be a member of top management. In my opinion he should not. First, usually top management cannot be familiar with the myriad problems involved in the union proposals. These men do not do the preparation for negotiations, and they do not have the benefit of all of the discussions that have taken place prior to the negotiations. If they act as spokesman, they may well agree to something without full knowledge of the facts and the implications. Second, the union usually wants to involve the top decisionmaker of the company because he is used to making decisions, will make them, and from then on the issue is settled. But such a man usually does not have the patience of the professional negotiator who realizes that the timing of a concession is probably more important to the progress of the negotiation than the concession itself. If the company spokesman is at a level lower than top management, the negotiator has the opportunity to say, "We will have to study your proposal a little more and review it within the company." A more thorough consideration of the proposal can then take place. These are the basic objections to having top management negotiate. Additionally, at least in large corporations, top management could not devote the amount of time that is necessary to conduct negotiations. In a smaller company this may be possible.

The union spokesman may be either a local representative or an international representative. From the employer's point of view there are advantages and disadvantages in either arrangement. The international representative usually is more sophisticated in negotiations and may have a more realistic idea of what can be achieved. Usually, also, he is more inclined to influence the members of the union's negotiating team to lower their sights. On the other hand, the local representative usually has a better knowledge of local practices. The international representative frequently feels that employers are alike and that the settlement in any negotiation should be consistent with other contracts with other employers. United has prided itself on being unique in many respects. The company has felt that it should not adopt proposals from other contracts to correct improper actions by other management just to meet a so-called "industry standard." Instead, contracts should reflect and solve United's own problems. On occasions, this desire has come into conflict with the desire of international representatives to bring about uniformity of contract provisions.

The negotiating teams usually arrive at a common position outside the conference room. Our negotiations normally run from 10:00 A.M. until noon and from 2:00 P.M. until 4:00 P.M. After each negotiating session, the management team meets, discusses what happened in the negotiations, and tries to come to a consensus. If we are in negotiations and do not have a common position, we take a recess and caucus. No rule of negotiations requires immediate answers. Everyone understands that the entire negotiating team must come to a common approach. In my own experience, I do not recall any situation in which the management team did not have a common approach. We all see the necessity for saying one thing, the spokesman is the man who is going to say it, and we all agree on it.

Formalities of Negotiation

Certain formalities normally precede the start of collective bargaining. At the first meeting, we usually agree with the union on the schedule of negotiations in terms of hours of the day. We identify the spokesman for the company and the spokesman for the union. Management also generally makes a statement to the effect that we would like to follow our normal practice of disposing of the rules items before we talk about cost items. In other words, we divide the union's proposals and our proposals into two basic classifications: (1) rules items, which include hours of work, work classifications, etc., and (2) cost items, which include wages and fringe benefits. We indicate that we must dispose of the rules items because we cannot talk intelligently about wages and fringe benefits until we know the rules items are reduced to a point where there are no major costs in the outstanding rules proposals. For example, one union rules proposal might be for a paid meal period within the eight hours of a shift. In its effect, the proposal would reduce the work week from 40 hours to 37-1/2 hours. Obviously, we cannot talk intelligently about wages unless we know how much the company will get for those wages. Accordingly, we try to dispose of the rules items before going on to cost items.

Following these formalities, we normally have a review of all proposals of both the union and the company for the purpose of clarification and explanation. In this review, we do not go into the justification for the proposal. We try to pose specific factual situations to be sure that we know how the union's proposal is intended to apply. After the proposals have been clarified, we may have to make additional studies and additional analyses. Similarly, the union will ask questions to clarify the company's proposals.

As another formality we also state—and if we don't the union will—that anything we agree to is tentatively agreed to and is contingent upon reaching a satisfactory settlement on all items. This is a standard approach. It says, in effect, that if the union and the employer do not agree on everything, they have agreed on nothing. From an employer's standpoint, it makes sense. If the union insists on a high wage increase, the employer may not be able to hold to his tentative agreement on items in the rules area. From the union's standpoint, it also makes sense. The union may say that if the company is not willing to give something on certain rules, then the company must give more in the area of wages. So total agreement works both ways, and I think it is generally understood.

Employees, supervisors, and frequently the public show great interest in what goes on in negotiations on a day-to-day basis. In my opinion, however, holding public negotiations or issuing periodic progress reports are mistakes. This is a bargaining process. Sometimes it requires the negotiator to take positions that are relatively inflexible, perhaps with the full expectation that he may have to back off later on. It would not help to have these positions broadcast to the employees or to other levels of management so that they can be debated in the work areas by people who do not have all of the facts or know the continuity of the negotiation. Widespread publicity results in the negotiating teams taking formal positions rather than trying to solve the problem. Each becomes overly concerned about its public posture. This is especially true in management's case. Usually everything the union asks for is a benefit to the employees. If each management position responding to a union proposal is broadcast, the employees will have the feeling that the company is refusing to bargain. They will not understand that the result that comes out of this process will be satisfactory to them. There is, of course, nothing the employer can do about what the union tells the employees. I strongly feel, however, that either periodic communications by the company alone (which usually evoke a union reply) or a joint union-company release on the progress of the negotiations will hinder, rather than help, the negotiations. At crises times, however, when the negotiations have progressed well down the road to settlement, and decisions are being made that vitally affect both the employees and the company, we feel an obligation to inform the employees and all management levels of where the negotiations stand and why.

Some unions and companies have a court reporter make a stenographic transcript of the negotiations. While we have not tried this approach, I think the result would be to inhibit discussion and stop effective communication between parties who must communicate in order to reach agreement. We do have someone on our negotiating committee take notes, but these are simply a running record of the major points. We may refer to this record at a later time to determine what our intent was.

The Art of Bargaining

Experienced negotiators follow certain techniques that are generally recognized. These techniques are intended to accomplish the purpose of the negotiations, that is, to get a settlement. These techniques are not, however, universal tools. They are not adaptable to all negotiations. There is no such thing as a "typical" negotiation. Negotiations differ with the personalities of the people involved and the external pressures that bear upon the negotiating teams. These pressures include the influence of government, the economic climate, the union's political situation, the employer's financial situation, the employees' attitudes, and other factors of which the negotiator may not even be aware. Similarly, there is no such thing as a "standard" negotiation procedure. In one negotiation, certain techniques will be successful; in another, the same techniques may hinder rather than help to bring about a settlement. Accordingly, a negotiator may have to take an entirely different approach in one negotiation than he would in another. But there are certain things that I think are basic. First of all, in collective bargaining the negotiator is trying to persuade. He is attempting to bring about a settlement through voluntary action of the other party. He is trying to induce in the other party a willingness to agree on a basis that he thinks is reasonable. Since the negotiator is attempting to influence individuals, he should try to find out as much as he can about the type of people he is dealing with, how they think, and what their customary approach is. Obviously, a negotiator would deal in quite different ways with a representative of the other party whose word cannot be believed than with someone in whom he had complete confidence.

Another thing to keep in mind is that every move that the negotiator makes should be coldly and calculatedly designed to advance toward a settlement. Never make a move unless it will help to bring about a final settlement. Frequently not making a concession helps more than making the concession. Making concessions too readily leads to the false impression that the result is going to be much higher than the employer may be prepared to go. Each concession should be timed as a step toward the final settlement. So keep the end in sight.

Fundamental in negotiations is the avoidance of "siege" positions. The company may say that a particular subject is a matter of principle, and it does not make concessions on matters of principle. Similarly, the union may insist upon its demand without any modification. When such a statement is made, the die is cast, and bargaining room is limited. We at United rarely talk about "management prerogatives." It is like running up a red flag. I do not mean to imply that the employer must be prepared to make concessions on all points. At United there are a number of subjects that we feel are vital to the management and operation of the business. On these things I am sure that we would take a strike. We do not, however, discuss them in terms of "management prerogatives." We try to indicate a firm position on the basis of what we have to have in order to manage the business. We do not arbitrarily classify any subject as a management prerogative.

Stated in another way, the job of the negotiator is to maintain as much bargaining leeway as he can. He must try to avoid fixed positions. Thus, on some occasions in the late stages of negotiations, the union representative will say, "Is that your final offer?" The proper reply is a small smile and the cliché that death and taxes are the only sure things in this world. We add that the offer is one that is justified and warrants serious consideration.

A major part of each negotiation is an attempt to determine the size of the problem. Frequently an initial proposal is broad, sweeping, and costly. It cannot be accepted. The problem the proposal was aimed at correcting, however, may be relatively small. The solution is to dig until the problem is uncovered and then determine the facts and what can be done to prevent a reoccurrence. Contract proposals frequently have their source in the emotions of people. As may be imagined, negotiations on an emotional level are rarely successful. To the extent problems can be evaluated in the light of the facts, their settlement can be made easier.

Be alert for smoke signals. Smoke signals are a technique of negotiation that most experienced negotiators use. It is a way of telling the other side what you are willing to do to arrive at a settlement without making formal concessions in the process. For example, the union may propose an increase of 37¢ an hour. After extended discussion of the justification for 37¢ an hour, the union spokesman may say, "Our proposal is still 37¢ an hour, and the negotiating team can't go back to the membership unless it has a settlement that is fair and reasonable." When he indicates that a "fair and reasonable" settlement may be something other than 37¢ an hour, he is indicating a willingness to move off of that figure. It is the obligation of the management negotiator to give similar signals. In other words, if management were offering an increase of 5¢ an hour, the management spokesman may well say, "Our position is that 5¢ an hour is all that we can see at this time. We certainly can't do anything more when you are staying at 37¢ an hour." This is an indication to the union that management will increase its offer if the union will decrease its asking figure.

Silence has meaning. If the negotiating teams talk about a union proposal at length with no change in position and then, without any logical reason, the union team stops talking about the proposal, they may be indicating that the union will withdraw it. If management has a union proposal under study for an extended period without indicating a reaction, the union may believe that management is only waiting for an appropriate time to accept the proposal. On occasions, either party may be misled because the other did not keep an issue alive. From management's standpoint it is well to explain any long delays in indicating a reaction to a union proposal to avoid an inference that the proposal is being received favorably.

If the rules items have been reduced and the justification for the wage and fringe benefit proposals has been thoroughly covered, the normal order is to talk next about "package" proposals. In a package proposal the union or management will prepare a "total" offer, which includes everything they feel should be in a final settlement. Such a package has in it rules items previously agreed to, plus any additional rules items, a wage increase and any additional fringe benefits. When one party has made a package proposal, the other will normally reply in a package proposal. The process then is to try to get the packages closer and closer together rather than to talk about individual items. Management usually should make the first package proposal and it should be a substantial one. Hopefully, the management offer will then provide the basis for realistic further discussions. If the union makes the first package offer, it is usually necessary to get a considerable reduction in the package before management logically can make an offer.

At United, normally, we do not make unreasonably low wage offers with the idea of leaving a wide area to bargain upward. When the union gets such an offer from management, it knows it must reply in kind, and negotiation is drawn out while each party slowly haggles toward the settlement area. Even more damaging, however, is the fact that the union can use management's first offer to take a strike vote. If the union is unwilling to move to a reasonable position, it is a better procedure to tell its representatives that the union expectations are so much greater than management can see resulting from the negotiations that management does not feel it can make a proposal. In other words, we try to get the union to reduce their position to the point that we can justify making a counter proposal. Then the negotiators go through the inching process of the union reducing their proposal a little more; management increases its offer a little more; and this continues until they come to the settlement point. Negotiations, however, are not a game of checkers. The fact that the union makes a modification of its position does not mean that management must make a move, and vice versa. The employer negotiator should not make any move unless he feels that it will induce further movement by the union. Usually the union will call attention to the fact that it has withdrawn many of its proposals while the company has not made corresponding concessions. The answer, of course, is that when management makes a move it is giving up dollars; when the union makes a move it is giving up "blue sky."

Knowledge of negotiating techniques and even negotiations experience cannot substitute for the judgment and sensitivity to other people that mark the successful negotiator. Such a person realizes that part of his job is to try to look at the problem from the point of view of the people on the other side of the table—not just to present and maintain a position. He must look at them not necessarily as they are but as they see themselves. He must try to determine what they really expect to accomplish in the negotiations and guide the negotiations toward that goal if it is achievable. If it is not, he must try to establish more realistic goals in the minds of the individuals on the other side. To do this, he needs some insight into the desires and expectations of the other negotiating committee. I do not believe that I can ever see things in precisely the same way as a union representative although I try my best within my limitations. This was illustrated to me in a negotiation last fall. When we were telling the union "no" with some degree of regularity, the union spokesman finally said, "If you persist in your position, I am going to have to talk to the Great White Father in Mecca." I thought he was referring to United's chairman of the board. In fact, he was referring to the president of the international union. The incident clearly illustrated to me that each of us looks at the world with a different set of eyes.

Mediation As an Aid to Bargaining

The use of a mediator to help the union and the employer reach agreement takes the place of a good negotiating relationship. Ideally, in negotiations the spokesmen for each party should try to understand each other and be able to communicate their views of what the settlement should be. If, however, communication during negotiations has broken down, a mediator can be helpful. The union and management offers may be so far apart that neither party is willing to make a move toward a realistic settlement area. The mediator tries to determine what the union's rock bottom figure is as well as the company's highest offer. He then tries to persuade the parties to come to agreement. If the parties have confidence in the mediator's integrity and judgment, they may indicate to him positions that they would not be willing to indicate openly to each other. In these situations, the neutrality of the mediator helps to overcome the communications block.

Types of Union-Management Relationships

As stated at the outset, a contract negotiation is only one expression of an over-all union-management relationship. Union-management relationships may, rather arbitrarily, be classified into three major categories.

Have Armed Truce

The principal characteristic of the "armed truce" type of union-management relationship is that the union is considered a necessary evil. In such an environment, the union feels it must challenge every management action affecting employees in order to indicate its power to the membership. There is fundamental disagreement over the scope of collective bargaining. The union usually wishes to enlarge the area in which its voice is heard; management tried to limit the subjects that it feels are proper matters for union-management discussion. Management also jealously protects the responsibility for managing the business. Management and the union vie for the worker's loyalty. Basically, economic power rather than reason, argument, and compromise determine the contract settlement.

Work in Harmony

In a "work in harmony" relationship the union is considered an asset as well as a liability. It provides an upward channel of communication to convey to management employee attitudes and com-

61

plaints that the employee is not willing to tell his supervisor. The union believes that the attainment of its objectives depends on the continuing prosperity and well-being of the company. Both the union and the company know that they can, and must, compromise so that each of their interests can be attained. The management retains the responsibility of running the business while the union confines its activities to vigilant policing of the agreement. There is a tendency to broaden the scope of matters subject to joint discussion and negotiation. Management enhances the union's prestige by involving it in a wider range of matters affecting employees. Both the union and the company recognize the complexity of the internal problems of the other and have a willingness to work out a reasonable and practical solution.

Work in Cooperation

Union-management cooperation is the third type of management relationship. It is relatively rare in the United States. In this relationship, management believes the union is willing, and able, to organize the employees to achieve lower costs and increased efficiency. It, therefore, is willing to share vital managerial functions with the union. The union is eager to boost production in return for benefits to itself and its members. The parties are able to work together with mutual trust and respect.

The union-management relationship in any enterprise at any one point in time is determined by the personalities of the union and management people involved, the environment of the enterprise, and the attitude employees have toward their job. One company and one union may progress from the armed-truce type of relationship to the work-in-harmony type of relationship. As management and union leaders and objective factors change, the relationship may retrogress or progress. What is sure is this: <u>Contract negotiations between the union and management will be an expression of their existing relationship.</u>

Conclusion

Collective bargaining is simply one facet of the total personnel function. It is perhaps the most dramatic facet, but it is not independent of the employer's over-all personnel policies. The collective bargaining relationship that exists between an employer and his employees, what the proposals will be in contract negotiations, and the difficulties the employer will have in arriving at a settlement are influenced by many factors that are controllable in the personnel function. The type of employees that are hired, the training given employees, and how employees are handled in terms of advising them of the decisions that affect them; all strongly influence the collective bargaining relationship. Accordingly, collective bargaining offers an opportunity to implement the employer's personnel policy. It gives to the individual in personnel work an excellent opportunity to participate in decisions that have an immediate and long-lasting effect. It enables the personnel man to help condition the employee's attitude toward his employer. It is a challenging job.

7.

Employee Grievance Procedures

John E. Massey

Because of my personal experience, my discussion of employee grievance procedures will deal principally with those for unionized employees. In addition, it will draw heavily on TVA practice, for I have been a TVA employee since 1936.

The Tennessee Valley Authority was created in 1933. Early in its development TVA recognized a number of international unions of the AFL-CIO as representing its trades and labor employees. Since 1937 it has dealt with these unions through the Tennessee Valley Trades and Labor Council. Since 1940 it has operated under a comprehensive written agreement with the Council, which at present is made up of 16 AFL-CIO international unions.

TVA white-collar employees are also unionized. Between 1941 and 1943 TVA recognized several international unions of the AFL-CIO and two independent unions as representing most white-collar employees below the management level. Since 1943 the TVA has dealt with these unions through the Salary Policy Employee Panel. Since 1950 it has had a comprehensive written agreement with the Panel. Agreements with both the Council and the Panel include a grievance procedure.

At the present time 90 per cent of TVA's positions are in bargaining units represented by the organizations that make up the Council and the Panel. The remaining 10 per cent are mostly positions that TVA considers ineligible for representation because of management responsibilities.

Legal Framework for Collective Bargaining

The experience of the Tennessee Valley Authority differs from that of most public agencies because by law it was not subject to the provisions of civil service laws or to regulations or other supervision of a civil service commission. The TVA Board of Directors was given complete authority and responsibility for personnel matters, subject only to the provisions (1) that neither a member of the Board nor any employee of the Board may permit or give consideration to any political test or qualification in the selection of employees, and (2) that laborers and mechanics shall be paid not less than the rates prevailing in the vicinity for similar work. This legal framework made full collective bargaining possible since TVA was not limited in negotiations to what was left over from the matters covered by civil service laws and regulations.

With the passage of the years, however, laws have been enacted that apply to certain personnel activities of TVA, and responsibility for implementing these laws—through issuance and enforcement of regulations—was assigned to the U.S. Civil Service Commission. These laws and these regulations have, of course, reduced the scope of collective bargaining in TVA. They have also made certain TVA personnel actions subject to appeal to the Commission.

Role of Civil Service Commissions in Grievances

Now, a civil service commission is not like an arbitrator. An arbitrator, hopefully at least, is a disinterested party. On the other hand, when a commission is hearing an appeal, it is passing on the application by an operating agency of regulations issued by the commission pursuant to law. It is enforcing its own regulations.

Also, a civil service commission is not an integral part of management, as is the personnel department of a private business. While many commissions have taken a positive role in personnel administration and have become to a degree an arm of management, they are not in a position to be an integral part of management. They have a legal existence independent of management. Moreover, historically, they were established as the protector of job applicants and employees against political favoritism by management, and they are now regarded by employees as the protector of a number of employee rights. Incidentally, some unions of government employees seem to consider it an advantage to apply more-or-less continuous pressure on the commissions. Of course, some other organizations with a considerable population of government employees as members—veterans' organizations, for example—do the same. Thus, civil service commissions are likely to have a dual loyalty—to management, on the one hand, and to employees, on the other. This arrangement has endured for many years and may have its advantages. It is, however, a different arrangement than is found in private business.

Thus, in talking about grievance procedures in the public service, we have to consider that for grievances on certain matters there is a factor not found in private industry practice; namely: Appeal beyond the agency to a body which traditionally has a role as protector of employees, and which, in hearing the appeal, is enforcing its own regulations.

We have not in TVA been able as yet to evaluate fully the significance of this appeal factor as it relates to grievance procedures. I think, however, there is some feeling within management that if a matter is appealable to the U.S. Civil Service Commission and that Commission can make a binding decision, then (1) the employee will exercise his right to appeal to the Commission if he does not get the answer he wants under the agency grievance procedure; and (2) it is doubtful that there is any advantage to management in trying to induce the employee to carry his case through more than the initial step of the agency grievance procedure.

While as yet our ideas about how a provision for appeal to a commission might influence the design of a grievance procedure are rather foggy, we are much clearer as to how it influences the effectiveness of a union-management relationship. In brief, it weakens such a relationship in proportion to the number of types of matters that are appealable. But this is another matter.

Why Have a Grievance Procedure?

Why have a grievance procedure in a nonunionized agency? In private industry a procedure might have been established for one, or both, of the following reasons:

1. To help prevent or delay unionization.

2. Because the upward communication of employee complaints makes for a healthier organization. If not expressed to his supervisor in words, an employee's dissatisfaction will be expressed in undesirable actions, such as careless work, reduced productivity—planned or unplanned—or passing on to other employees distorted views which have an adverse morale effect. John Pfiffner has noted, that if the supervisor is a good listener, the grievance sometimes vanishes in the telling, and sometimes the employee comes up with his own solution to the problem.

A nonunionized public agency has an additional reason for having a grievance procedure. It will provide a channel for complaints which, hopefully, employees will use in preference to appealing to their elected representatives in the legislature. A public agency that deals with its employees through unions will find that the negotiated grievance procedure can be very effective in this respect. Most employees realize that the typical legislator has a degree of confidence in the effectiveness of a grievance procedure under a collective bargaining contract; the legislator will expect the employee to utilize the grievance procedure and will respect the decision which is produced by the procedure.

Any organization that has recognized a union as the collective bargaining agent for some or all of its employees that are eligible for representation knows that the grievance procedure is a basic element in the collective bargaining contract.

1. It provides the means by which differences of opinion about the proper application of negotiated procedures in specific instances may be worked out.

2. It is the means by which individual misunderstandings can be cleared up before they turn into burning issues involving large groups of employees.

3. In some instances, the grievance procedure is a means of settling individual complaints about matters not mentioned in the collective bargaining agreement. This might be called "negotiating in miniature." In fact, there is some negotiation in miniature in all grievances under a union contract.

Steps in a Grievance Procedure

What are the steps in an effective grievance procedure? The first step, it seems to me, is discussion with the immediate supervisor. By this I mean the responsible supervisor—not a lead-man or a straw boss. Most grievances can, and should, be settled at this point.

In TVA the second step is appeal to the division director. A division is a major subdivision of TVA, and a division director reports to the General Manager. At this step a hearing is usually held, and a verbatim record is made and submitted to both employee and management representatives for approval as to accuracy. All facts about the grievance are supposed to be presented at the hearing, and the record is the basis of decision at this and any subsequent steps. Ordinarily the division director is not present at the hearing. A hearing officer named by the director conducts the hearing. The director makes his decision from the record.

At one time the TVA grievance procedure provided for appeal through each step in the supervisory line from the immediate supervisor all the way to the division director. This arrangement was discarded many years ago. For an excellent discussion of the weaknesses of this kind of a procedure see Effective Procedures for the Handling of Employee Grievances by Louis J. Van Mol, who is now General Manager of TVA. This monograph, published in 1953 by the Public Personnel Association, is one of the classics in the literature on grievance procedure.

Should there be an appeal within the agency beyond the division director, that is, beyond the director of the major subdivision of an agency? Or should the division director make the final agency decision?

In the nonunionized agency, or for grievances by nonrepresented employees, there is merit, it seems to me, in having the division director's decision be the final agency decision. He is in a position where he should be able to take into account all agency interests. Since some may disagree with this view and think the agency head or the director of personnel should render the final decision, I should say that there is as yet no definite conclusion on this point in TVA. There have been very few grievances by employees who are not eligible for union representation.

When there is a negotiated grievance procedure, it seems to me that the management official who is responsible for negotiating the collective bargaining agreement should be responsible for making the final agency decision in grievances. This official may be the agency head himself; or as in TVA, he may be the director of personnel; or in some organizations he may be the director of industrial relations. In any event, he is the official responsible for overseeing the development and maintenance of an effective relationship with the union. In arriving at a decision in a grievance he can, and should, take into consideration the impact of the decision on all the elements of this relationship.

In TVA's negotiated grievance procedures there is a provision whereby the union or the director of personnel may request a conference before a final decision is rendered. The conference is attended by the top representative of the union involved, one or more representatives of the Council or Panel, the division director, and the director of personnel. The principal value of this conference is that it may clarify for both union and management the extent to which and the manner in which the over-all union-management relationship is involved in the particular grievance. We are now considering experimenting with predecision conferences of this type at the division director level. We would hope that such conferences would help to avoid a tendency of both management and union to draw a hard line at this point—a "here we stand and fight" attitude.

Time Limits in Grievances

What about time limits in processing grievances? Grievances should be settled promptly, of course. If they are not, the feeling of dissatisfaction behind a grievance may grow and spread to employees not directly involved. Paul Pigors and Charles A. Myers have pointed out that failure to deal promptly with even a trifling matter may contribute to an impression that management does not care how workers feel. An employee may brood over such a matter and magnify its significance. If he broods long enough, his preoccupation with the matter may blot out all his more favorable impressions of the company. Moreover, dissatisfactions are communicated among employees during lunch and rest periods, in the washroom, and on the job, and they lose nothing in the telling.

Most grievance procedures set time limits for each step. TVA's agreement with the Trades and Labor Council requires the employee to take up a grievance with the responsible supervisor within 10 calendar days from the date of the action, or notice of proposed action, with which he is dissatisfied. The supervisor must give him an answer within 10 days. The employee has 10 days to appeal the supervisor's answer to his division director. The division director must render a decision within three weeks after he receives the corrected transcript of the hearing. If the employee wishes to appeal to the director of personnel, he must do so within 10 days, and so on.

These time limits might be considered overly generous by some organizations. However, they have been satisfactory for TVA, whose employees are stationed at many different locations away from division headquarters and from local union headquarters; as necessary, they have been extended by mutual agreement. In addition to the geographical factor, these time limits also recognize that a job steward may need to consult with a heavily burdened business agent located several hundred miles away. Likewise, a supervisor may wish to seek advice or information from his headquarters before giving a grieving employee an answer to his complaint.

Even where an agency is small and at one location, and where the principal union representative is readily available, sufficient time should be allowed for the employee and his union representative to think through the case. Time for thinking may lead to a decision not to file a grievance, or at least it may lead to a grievance presentation in which the problem is clearly defined.

Considerations of this sort caused the Salary Policy Employee Panel to negotiate out most of the time limits in its agreement with TVA. Where there are no time limits the agreement provides that "employees, unions, and representatives of management are nevertheless expected to act promptly." This arrangement seems to be working about as well as the trades and labor agreement with its specific time limits. So, what about time limits? Are they necessary? And if so, what should they be?

Arbitration

What about arbitration? TVA has it, and the arbitrator's decision is binding. But we do not call it arbitration, and it is a little different from arbitration. We call it "referring a case to an im-

partial referee." And the impartial referee in a considerable proportion of the cases makes his decision on the basis of the record
developed within the agency. He can call for a hearing if he wishes
clarification of the record. A hearing is also held if either TVA or
the Trades and Labor Council requests one.

Is it better for a decision to be made with or without a hearing
before the referee? We have not decided. What is your view?

How does a case get to the impartial referee? In TVA an individual employee cannot have a case referred to a referee; neither
can an individual union. Only the Salary Policy Employee Panel or
the Trades and Labor Council can do this. Why have such an arrangement?

The reason for not permitting the individual employee to take
his case to the referee is that, at this stage, a grievance is not an
individual matter but a matter of relationship between TVA and the
union. Both TVA and the union have put forth considerable effort to
secure all the facts about the case and to reach a solution acceptable to both parties. Now they have reached a point where they cannot agree but seemingly can do no more themselves. Both parties
need a final resolution of the matter so that they can get on to other matters. The referee provides this final resolution.

The reason for the provision that only the Panel or the Council, and not an individual union, can take a grievance to a referee
is that referring a matter to an outsider for final settlement is not
an action that should be taken lightly. Both management and union
give up some element of control in this action. Accordingly, the individual union must be able to persuade the entire Panel or the entire Council, as the case may be, that more is to be gained as far
as both the individual question and the over-all relationship are
concerned than may be lost by going to a referee.

Should the grievance procedure exclude certain types of complaints? Should the types of grievances that may be appealed to an
impartial referee be limited? Clearly, a grievance procedure
should not be used for the purpose of changing an established standard, procedure, or provision of a negotiated agreement. Such
changes should be made through negotiation. Aside from this, under
the TVA grievance procedure an employee may file a grievance
(1) if he believes he has been treated unfairly, or (2) if he disagrees
with his supervisors as to the application of a policy to him as an
employee. Within the scope discussed above, the decision of the director of personnel in any grievance is appealable to the referee.

There is some risk in this kind of an arrangement. The union
could use it to secure modifications of established practice or procedure. However, the arrangement is consistent with TVA's over-

all approach to labor-management relations, which may be summarized as follows:

1. The successful performance of TVA's missions depends to a large degree on mutual understanding and unity of purpose between employees and management.

2. Such mutual understanding and unity can best be maintained if employees and management share in forming and administering the policies and rules that govern the relations between them and if there is ease of communication between them.

3. Responsible, recognized unions make it possible for employees to be more effective participants and to communicate with greater ease than they can as individuals.

TVA management expects the unions to represent employees in a statesmanlike manner; expects them not to seek short-run gains at the expense of long-run relationships; expects them to fully recognize and accept the mutual interdependence of union and management. The unions expect the same thing of TVA management. I know that at times each is disappointed in the other. However, as long as each makes a constant effort to find and cultivate mutual interests, I think TVA can afford to continue its wide-open grievance procedure. Time will tell if this is wishful thinking.

The managers of some public agencies may not be disposed to be so hopeful and may want to limit the types of grievances that may go to a referee.

A principal reason for doing so is fear that the referee's decision will in effect rewrite a part of the contract. A possible alternative to a limiting provision would be to provide in the contract that the referee's decision apply only to the specific grievance; that it will not control the application of contract terms to future job situations; that it may not be used as a precedent in arguing or deciding future grievances. Does this alternative seem to have any merit?

What about provision for arbitration of grievances of nonrepresented employees? This question assumes, of course, that there is a grievance procedure applicable to such employees—which is by no means universally the case. A survey of private companies published several years ago revealed that less than one-quarter of the companies had a written grievance procedure for unorganized employees, and only eight per cent reported provision for arbitration.

I believe that in the public field formal grievance procedures applicable to unorganized employees are more common but that binding arbitration of grievance decisions is almost never provided for. A 1964 survey by Man and Manager, Inc. revealed that 71 per cent of state, county, and municipal agencies polled had formal grievance procedures; however, the survey report did not distinguish between organized and unorganized employees. TVA does not provide for arbitration of a grievance as an individual employee right, even if his position is in a bargaining unit. So far as I know, the possibility of arbitrating a grievance of a nonrepresented employee has not even been officially considered in TVA.

Participation of Union Representatives in Grievances

What about participation of union representatives at each of the steps in a grievance? In a grievance under a negotiated procedure the union has a stake in the matter and is entitled to be present. The fact that the grieving employee may not be a union member or may not want the union to represent him is immaterial. The union is present as a representative of all employees in the bargaining unit who may be affected by the terms of settlement of a grievance. TVA agreements provide that the local union representative is notified when a grievance is appealed beyond the immediate supervisor. This assures that the union has an opportunity to be present at the second step in the procedure. It does not, however, mean that the union representative is not entitled to be present at the first step.

Who may represent the employee in a grievance under a negotiated grievance procedure? The TVA agreement with the Trades and Labor Council provides that the employee may represent himself or he may be represented by the union which has jurisdiction over his position. He may not be represented by a person other than the authorized union representative. This is in accord with the basic concept that a negotiated grievance procedure is a fundamental element in the relationship between management and the recognized union. A union would not have recognition as the exclusive representative of the employees in a bargaining unit if some other union or other type of organization could represent an employee in a grievance. The TVA agreement with the Salary Policy Employee Panel currently permits such outside representation, but negotiations are in process to remove this permissive arrangement from the contract. The rule went into the contract at a time when formal recognition of white-collar unions in government was very much an uncharted area.

Attitudes of Supervisors in Grievances

It is safe to say, I think, that a supervisor's attitude toward the grievances that come to him for handling will be a reflection of his

72

attitude toward the entire union-management relationship. If he regards the union as "the enemy," his hostility will "come through"
to the grieving employee and the union representative.

If he is the immediate supervisor, he will try to give the employee the brush-off. He will say, "I don't have time now to listen to
you." Or he will say, "We'll talk about it later," but does not schedule such a talk. If he does finally arrange to talk to the employee,
he will be an impatient listener. He will make it clear that he does
not understand why the employee is taking up his valuable time on
such a trifling matter. He will listen to the employee or the union
representative only to be able to refute what is said. He will be in-
dignant about statements which may indicate that he is not running
a bang-up operation—that there may be some human relationships
that could use a bit of attention. He will not sense the underlying
human need the employee is trying to express through grieving
about some specific incident.

If the supervisor is the division head, he will have similar reactions when he reads the record of a grievance in order to arrive
at a decision. The employee will not be present to sense them, but
when the decision is rendered the employee will read the carefully
prepared defensive statements and will know that nobody listened.
Such a division head will keep to the fore the concept of the solidar-
ity of the management team. The idea that the team that gets the
work done is an employee-management team is an idea which he
may verbally express but does not inwardly feel. Such a division
head, after reading the hearing record, will not go back to the immediate supervisor and say, "Let's talk this case over and make
sure that we know what the employee is telling us." No, he will not
consider doing this. He will render a decision upholding the immediate supervisor. If the immediate supervisor is going to be reversed, somebody else—the director of personnel, or the impartial
referee—will have to take the responsibility.

By contrast, there is the supervisor who regards the union as
an organization that provides a service to him under an agreement
or contract. It is a very special service that cannot be obtained just
anywhere and anytime. It is a service whose provision requires a
stable, continuing, and open-minded relationship. Such a supervisor
will look upon a grievance, particularly a grievance supported by
the union, as an attempt to bring to his attention a condition that
may impair the employee-management team effort. He will consider it worth his time to listen. He will hear what is said. He will ask
questions to learn as much about the condition as he possibly can.

Of course an individual supervisor—or division head—does not
exist in isolation apart from other supervisors, or apart from the
head of the agency. He will constantly observe what other super-

visors and division heads do and what the agency head does in matters involving the union-management relationship. What he sees them do, not what he hears them say, will affect his attitudes in handling a grievance, as well as his other relationships with the union.

The supervisor will also constantly observe the union in action. Does the union regard management as "the enemy"? Does it have the attitude that management is always taking advantage of employees? Unfortunately, some union representatives think this way, or they act this way because they think their members expect them to act this way. The supervisor who faces such a union representative in a grievance may experience a temporary increase in his blood pressure. But he is still well-advised to listen patiently and listen well. Unfortunately, in this type of situation he is on trial and must to some extent act accordingly. He cannot act with full effectiveness as a partner with the union in a search for enlightenment and mutual understanding about a common problem.

Training Supervisors and Union Representatives

The idea of partnership in searching for solutions to common problems can, and should, be cultivated among both supervisors and union representatives, with benefits to both management and union. It can be done through individual contacts by informed supervisors and union representatives. Organized training of both supervisors and union representatives in this idea could be helpful. Participation of the union in training supervisors and participation of management in training job stewards might be fruitful in getting across the idea of mutuality even in grievances. In TVA we have not done much training in grievance handling in recent years, but our thoughts are turning more and more in this direction, and I believe action will be forthcoming.

TVA has, however, been working intensively on the idea of mutuality through joint employee-management cooperative committees and conferences. Currently there are 99 such committees and conferences that are made up of local management and of employees designated by local unions. Most of these groups meet monthly and work from a jointly prepared agenda. They encourage and review suggestions on ways to improve job performance, increase safety, improve work environment, and promote training. They also are a channel for keeping employees informed about the TVA program and about local job progress; conversely, they are a channel for keeping management informed about employee thinking. They do not deal with individual grievances, but from working together in a cooperative program, the participants come to understand each other's points of view. This may well prevent grievances.

Summary

The contribution which a negotiated grievance procedure can make to teamwork on the job depends on the attitudes of those who have negotiated it and on the attitudes of their representatives who use it or administer it. Hopefully, enlightened and self-disciplined democracy will increasingly prevail in both union and management so that grievance procedures, as well as other parts of union-management relations, can make an increasing contribution to our society.

8. Role of Staff Agencies in Employee Relations

One of the truisms relating to the field of public personnel administration is that, with regard to techniques and practices, no two agencies do anything exactly the same way. This truism also holds with respect to the handling of employee relations. The situations that exist in different jurisdictions vary widely. The levels of government can range from a federal department to a township or borough. Some agencies are large; some are small. The organization of the management function is usually different for each level of government. Even at the same level, variations of standard patterns are common. To add to the confusion, there are many different titles for substantially the same position.

Another consideration that must be taken into account is the degree of sophistication and/or experience in management-employee relations that exists in a particular governmental jurisdiction. This sophistication or experience may range from a negative bias to a positive, well-established industrial type labor-management program that includes appendages such as contracts, union shop, arbitration, etc.

Because of such differences in the characteristics and the status of employee relations in each locality, I intend to discuss the activity on a generalized basis. Those readers who wish to be informed against the day when their employees may become organized as well as those who are looking for answers to current questions will need to adopt the methods and experiences to which I will refer, for few of them can be applied universally. On the other hand, in the reasoning, in the roles suggested, in the manipulation of influences and factors to cause established patterns or examples, there will often be suggestions to the way in which it may apply to a particular situation.

Before I begin to discuss the employee relations roles played by various staff agencies and their personnel I would like to comment briefly on the extent of the formality of those roles. In smaller cities employee relations may be handled on a very informal basis. There may be, for example, no need nor desire for a contract; if there is a contract, there may be no need for extensive contract language. In a jurisdiction where the status of management-employee relations is still in the developmental stage, both management

and labor may want to "play it by ear" for a while. Most larger jurisdictions will have developed a rather high degree of sophistication and formality in the conduct of their management-employee
relations. This will be especially true if there are multiple bargaining units, for with succeeding years, annual negotiations will have
resulted in refinement and continuing revision of the original labor
relations agreements.

The decision as to who is to handle management-employee
relations for the governmental organization can be extremely varied. It will depend (1) on the level and character of the level of government involved, (2) the organization of the management and/or
legislative function, and (3) the personalities and influences involved. In industry, management-employee relations are usually
handled by an industrial relations unit that may, or may not, include personnel. No particular pattern exists in government.

My discussion of management-employee relations in the public service will cover the contribution of the personnel director
and the departmental personnel officer as well as the roles of four
staff agencies—the central personnel agency; the fiscal agency; the
legal agency; and the public relations agency. The relationships
and responsibilities of these staff agencies with the executive and
legislative branches and line departments will also be considered.
Finally, I want to make it clear that my remarks are predicated on
the assumption that we are dealing with governmental jurisdictions
where management formally recognizes and negotiates with employee organizations.

Role of the Central Personnel Agency

The changing status of the personnel agency in government
concerning employee relations is aptly stated in the 1960 edition
of Municipal Personnel Administration, and I quote in part:

"The growing activity and influence of employee unions in
the public service has been an important factor in expanding
the role of the personnel agency from its traditional recruitment, examining, and related functions into the field of employee relations. It has been a major factor too in bringing the
personnel agency from its traditional relatively isolated position into a closer working relationship with line management,
. . .

"There has been growing recognition in the public service that employee relations affects virtually all major determinations of policy and operating program results. This has
long been recognized in private industry where the role of the

personnel or industrial relations department in performing research and giving specialized advice and guidance as a basis
for executive and supervisory decisions affecting personnel is
well established. An increasing number of municipal personnel
agencies are performing this function."

It cannot be denied that there is an increase in employee relations activities in the public service. It needs to be remembered,
however, that the authority or organization of the personnel agency
may, or may not, permit it to administer, or to be involved in, a
formal program of employee relations. In a number of jurisdictions,
the authority of the personnel agency extends no further than that of
administering an examination and classification plan together with
a few minor personnel policies. Such an agency cannot take on labor-management relations unless it is granted the responsibility by
some other arm of the service. This possibility is not likely to become a reality.

In contrast, a central personnel agency that embraces a considerable number of programs dealing with employment might very
well, and in my judgment should, take on the responsibility for the
labor-management program. Employment activities should be combined in one unit. Only an agency with adequate authority can ensure that any formal labor-management policy or practice is consistent with other employee or merit system provisions or policies.

In the event that a central personnel agency operating under an
established merit system takes on the responsibility for handling a
formally recognized management-employee relations program, the
question often arises as to the possible conflict of inimical interests and authority. I see no reason why this should be so. Except
for one phase of the selection process, all of the programs in a
comprehensive public personnel system are the counterparts of an
industrial personnel system. Recruitment, promotions, classification, wage administration, leave, training, safety, pensions, and
even testing are industrial-type programs. The only feature peculiar to a merit or civil service system is but the first of the three
fundamental principles of a civil service system: (1) the right of
any qualified person to compete for a position in the governmental
jurisdiction. Let's not fool ourselves that the other two merit system principles—(2) the right of tenure and (3) the right of appeal—
are unique to the public service. The unionized employee in private
industry also has tenure, and he has also well established his right
of appeal.

I repeat, I see no reason why a merit system agency cannot
administer a formal employee relations program. Let me use the
Philadelphia situation as an example. By civil service regulations,
labor agreements negotiated and entered into by the personnel di-

rector are "subject to the provisions of the Philadelphia Home Rule Charter and applicable regulations and statutes." Every provision in the city's contract with the AFL-CIO, with but two exceptions, is included in the Civil Service Regulations.

Again, let me quote from Municipal Personnel Administration.

"The personnel agency has a vital contribution to make to the shaping of general policy, whether by administrative or legislative action. In this role the personnel agency, particularly if it contains a specialized employee relations staff, becomes the repository not only of technical knowledge of the subject matter of personnel administration but also of such knowledge and experience [as is needed to deal with organized employees]. . . . It will be aware of the conditions of success of the various approaches to collective dealing, of the bases and tested methods for assuring sound and workable settlement of questions of representation, of the probable effects of any possible limitations on the types of employee representatives who are recognized, and the scope of subjects appropriate for various types of joint union-management discussion.

"Another type of service which the personnel agency is being called upon to render when policies are being established lies in the area of method. It has become increasingly common for the personnel agency to take an active part in negotiations and, in some cases, to assume a role of representative of the executive in working out agreements, subject to such executive and legislative ratification as is necessary."

Depending on the legislative or quasi-legislative authority the personnel agency may possess, it may, of course, adopt or recommend any agreed to labor-management policies. Depending on the jurisdiction, the acceptance could vary from legislation, administrative order, or memorandum of understanding.

When a merit system agency undertakes collective dealing with management-employee matters, the individual employee's rights are almost always preserved. This is usually one of management's interests which it establishes early in negotiations, or else legislation requires this protection. Additionally, the employee's rights of appeal are usually basic in the merit system law against dismissals, suspensions, and demotions, and in which the employee organization almost without exception will represent the employee.

When the public personnel system is not under a merit system, the rights of individual employees will undoubtedly all be subject to negotiation. Areas in which the services of the personnel agency can and should be helpful in implementing a management-employee relations program and negotiations include comprehensive data and wage gathering; analysis and interpretation of subjects appropriate for labor negotiation; research; submitting recommendations relating to existing—or proposed—practices, policies, or employee benefits; training of supervisors in employee relations; and development of personnel management policies and procedures.

Theory and practice may vary as to the character and degree of relationships and responsibilities of the central personnel agency with the executive and legislative branches and line departments. The situation will depend to a considerable extent on the concept and authority of the agency. But if the personnel agency is to be a part of the employee relations program or is to play a major role, it had better be in the mainstream of activity with the executive and legislative branches. If the agency is headed by a civil service commission in addition to a personnel director, the commission must not only be informed as to the continuing status of the labor-management program activities; it must also be made aware of employee organization demands, progress in negotiations, and the probable outcome. The personnel director should keep the commission up to date on employee relations developments; the commission should, in turn, confer with the chief executive, management's negotiating team, and the legislative committee. Such conferences are necessary for the commission and its director to express their views and to reconcile any differences that may arise long before final agreement is reached with the employee organization. It is my opinion that the commissioners should not individually participate in the actual negotiations, but there would be no conflict of interest if they should do so.

Role of the Personnel Director

Based on my experience as a public personnel director for more years than I care to remember, I find it very easy to answer the question as to who the personnel director represents in management-employee relations activities. No question about it. He represents management.

The personnel man has been accused of wearing many different hats; frequently he's accused of wearing more than one at a time! But I see no conflict in his wearing the same hat for his role of management representative and his role as administrator of the merit system. When he is on the negotiating team, he may haggle, bargain, and compromise. But it is part of his job to discuss and consider employee requests presented by their representatives. When he administers the merit system, the grievance procedure, or any other part of the labor-management agreement, his job is to find out what is right, not who is right. He can wear all these hats and still be respected by employees and their representatives.

Someone has asked whether the personnel director should serve as a buffer, bluffer, or bargainer when he deals with employees and employee organizations.

I don't think the personnel director should be, or need be, a buffer. He has a much more important role to play. He should administer the labor agreement—on a continuing basis. He should carry it out, as agreed to by all, and if necessary confer and draw into any controversy, as partners, the other members of the management negotiating team.

The personnel director certainly should not try to be a bluffer. Never bluff nor break a commitment to a union; if you do, your effectiveness is at an end. However, there is absolutely no need to bluff. Each public personnel task, be it employee relations, classification, pay, selection or any other action should be approached and handled with the skill, competence, and preparation it deserves. Every personnel director should be ready to meet those problems on an informal and knowledgeable basis.

I do think the personnel director should be the public agency's bargainer. I also believe that he should be its labor relations expert. Labor relations is an important function in any organization. I think that the personnel director should be assigned to administer this function. And he must make sure that when he is called upon he has the necessary expertise. Employee relations is clearly related to the field of operations of the personnel director rather than to that of either the chief executive or finance director.

In industry the personnel men with the highest salaries and the greatest prestige are those who function mainly in the area of labor relations and union negotiations. Too many personnel practitioners are content to permit the personnel function to be relegated to a minor role, to accept the status quo as limited in the legislation, to become embroiled with a multitude of personnel techniques, devices, and gimmicks. Labor relations programs are rapidly increasing over the country, and the personnel director should be capable of rising to the occasion when management selects the unit or individual to handle this task. The personnel director needs to have rapport with top management, but he must have earned it beforehand. His competence and the regard held for him will in great measure determine his role.

It is admitted that labor relations entail considerable cost in time and talent. This activity imposes a strain on public authorities as well as on the employee organizations and requires wide knowledge of the labor scene and a skill of a highly particular nature. It appears, too, that many public officials fight against getting involved in the labor-management process.

If the personnel director is to become involved in employee relations, he must become a resource person. He must, through personal contact or correspondence with others, be responsible for obtaining extensive information concerning other governmental jurisdictions and business and industry. He must be thoroughly informed about the local labor market in which his organization is in competition. Studies must be undertaken to secure many kinds of statistics and to arrange for their presentation in convenient form. Wage surveys for the locality, and/or on a nation-wide basis for technical, professional, and administrative positions; studies of fringe items; and analyses of current practices with respect to leave, shift differentials, disciplinary patterns, mileage, premium pay, and hours of work are illustrative of these studies.

On the basis of his knowledge and the data he obtains, the personnel director is in a position to serve as an advisor to the personnel agency commission, if any, and also to top management. He can be the catalyst in directing the negotiating team by developing a unified understanding of what should be agreed to or the extent to which a compromise should be made on a "stalled" position. If not the catalyst, he certainly can provide recommendations based on facts and experience.

The personnel director should be charged with the responsibility of administering the labor-management agreement on a continuing basis. This is particularly true if he participated as a member of the negotiating team. The responsibility is a natural role for him. Let me repeat in part what I have previously written. First, since the personnel director administers the personnel system, he is thoroughly familiar with all of its policies and requirements. Second, since he has personally been involved in collective bargaining he will have been responsible for revising personnel policies in the light of any benefits granted. Lastly, his interpretations of contract clauses and personnel policies must tie in with the over-all planning.

The personnel director has, or should have, as one of his major responsibilities the maintenance and preservation of management's rights. This matter of rights for management can occur in two major areas. The first occurs at the bargaining table. Here is where the management of an organization may "give away" a benefit that is ill-advised or too liberal or costly in contrast with the benefits granted by its competitors in business or government. In maintaining management's rights, management should aim at preserving the freedom and authority to (1) control the flow of work; (2) make necessary changes in job content, work loads, and sched-

82

ules; (3) establish work standards; (4) introduce new equipment and methods; (5) eliminate useless jobs; and (6) allocate, lay off, discipline, and discharge employees on a fair, reasonable, and just basis.

The second area in which the personnel director should be concerned about maintaining and preserving management's rights is in the day-to-day administration of the labor agreement in the line departments. The personnel director must be constantly on the alert for actions that are departures from negotiated policy. If a supervisor permits informal actions to become precedent and then practice, they will become established policies as surely as though they were granted in formal negotiation.

As briefly as possible, I want to discuss the role of the personnel director if he is a member of the bargaining team that normally handles annual negotiations on employee organization requests. He shall surely prepare facts and arguments and participate in planning management's strategy in coping with employee requests. He certainly should personally engage in the give-and-take of the negotiations. Whether or not he is chairman of the management team, he should make major presentations at the bargaining table or deal with special areas of discussion in which he is particularly well equipped to handle.

Prior to, and during, the progress of the negotiations he shall keep his commission, if any, apprised of developments, confer with the other members of the bargaining team, as occasion demands, confer with the chief executive, managing director, finance director, president of city council, councilmanic finance committee, etc. This type of communication is always necessary to provide a "family understanding" of agreeing, management-wise, on what the employment benefit package shall be. Revisions of management's position often occur at these meetings through compromise, quid pro quos, or counterproposals.

In preparing for, or during, negotiations the personnel director individually develops, or obtains from others, alternate counterproposals to meet management's needs or to satisfy the employee organization. Counterproposals are for the purpose of getting back all, or part, of some undesirable benefit granted in the past; of meeting some unacceptable demand by the workers, either in part or by substitution, if possible, of another solution; and to gain acceptance of a program, again in whole or in part, which management would choose to have accepted.

83

Role of the Fiscal Agency

For a number of important reasons the finance director should be a member of the negotiating team—and a participating member, not just an observer. By his position he is a member of top management and, very likely, a member of the chief executive's cabinet. In these roles he is thoroughly familiar with the public pronouncements on what may or may not be done concerning labor-management agreements, and he has taken part in any off-the-record discussions.

It is part of the job of a finance director to constantly advise the chief executive and the legislative body of the current and projected status of the financial situation of the jurisdiction, and he must keep them informed as to any potential further financial demands on tax resources that would result from employee requests. It follows that his recommendations, either pro or con, are extremely important.

During negotiations, the finance director is in an excellent position to represent management's position relating to financial issues. He can point out also to the bargaining team in its pre-negotiating sessions what is, and what is not, possible in terms of availability of funds. Finally, he can defend the propriety of any agreed-to monetary benefit consummated with the employee organization by virtue of his participation in the bargaining process and his acceptance that the additional or liberalized benefit is financially feasible. This support can be extremely important in backing up an agreement by management's negotiating team, which if reversed by higher authority could be extremely embarrassing. It is not necessary to belabor the point that the influence of the legislative and executive arm of government determines, in great part, and for a variety of reasons, wages and fringe benefits granted to workers in a given jurisdiction.

The assistance available from the fiscal agency will depend upon the extent to which the agency is equipped to provide a variety of financial data. Fortunate indeed is the jurisdiction whose finance department processes payrolls by machine accounting. If payroll data are on cards or tapes the available information is almost limitless, complete, and accurate in analyzing and computing costs of requests. Almost as important is the fact that this information is available almost immediately and would cover all departments.

Illustrative of data that is usually available from the fiscal agency are the number of employees, their job classifications, the pay range and current pay step of each. Employee organization and dues check-off is also easily determined. The current annual cost of wages and of each existing fringe benefit can be quickly deter-

mined. In the same manner, the projected costs of proposed liberalized employee demands which may or are to be negotiated and
are of a montary nature can be readily computed on such items
as wage adjustments, overtime, stand-by time, shift differentials,
hours of work, mileage, insurance, pensions, and a variety of others.

Role of the Legal Agency

Undoubtedly, many jurisdictions about to embark on a program
of employee relations will want to know what role management's attorney should play. Lawyers often take an important part in union
negotiations in industry. Should management's solicitor in government take part in the negotiations? Should he, because of his training, be delegated chief negotiator? Should he be one of the negotiators? Should he simply serve as an observer?

Many unions abhor company attorneys more than nature ab-
hors a vacuum. This in itself may indicate how helpful some may
feel an attorney can be to management's cause. A stiff-necked attorney with a t-crossing and i-dotting mind can sometimes do more
harm than good. Thousands of industry negotiations have been handled without a lawyer participating either actively or as an observer. It must be recognized, however, that in many jurisdictions the
chief executive or chief administrative officer or the personnel director may want the solicitor to be at the bargaining table and to do
all of the drafting of the agreement language. This may be due to
their confidence in his advice, his competence, his ability to articulate and his personality. It is obvious, of course, that an attorney
who sits at the bargaining table—even as a silent observer—will
have a chance to get a first-hand feel of the intent of the parties.

The most common role of the solicitor in labor-management
relations is that of clarifier or interpreter of a host of questions.
The basic inquiries deal with possible conflicts of employee relations policies or agreements with merit system, state, or local
laws. In the absence of specific authorization, the solicitor must
rule on the legality of a proposal. For example, if management is
considering the establishment of an employee relations program
in a jurisdiction, he must determine whether or not there will be
any infringement on the individual employee's rights which may
have been granted in the past. There is the possibility of conflict
between civil service provisions and those incorporated in the labor agreement. Also to be considered is the priority of state versus local law versus civil service legislation versus what can be
legally adopted in a labor agreement.

The attorney must also decide whether a subject is appropriate, legally, for negotiation. Negotiations with a public agency under a merit system would normally not include such subjects as employee selection, the length of the probationary period, or disciplinary appeals. These personnel actions are usually covered by local or state legislation and thus would be legally excluded from consideration for inclusion in negotiations or labor agreement. Obviously, inclusions or exclusions of various subjects will depend on the locality. Considerable confusion exists on this point. Officials in different cities in the same state may disagree as to what can, or cannot, be negotiated. Not only may solicitors' opinions in different localities vary as to legality; court decisions may add to the problem.

Even in those jurisdictions where the solicitor is neither part of the negotiating team nor has responsibility for drafting new or revised clauses in the labor agreement, he or his staff should be required to review such language for legality, draftsmanship, inconsistencies, and errors. In the review of the final draft before adoption by a neutral, trained individual, an attorney is often able to point out a number of desirable improvements. In any case, no solicitor should be asked to review an agreed-upon contract 24 hours before it is to be signed. Minor suggestions may not be worth his concern, and the odds are that at that late date management would not be willing to open up negotiations to push for an important change he might suggest.

A recurring task that may be given to the solicitor in a jurisdiction with established management-employee relations is interpretation of the language contained in labor agreement clauses. Quite often when an effort is made to translate some provision of a labor agreement to on-the-job policy, a difference of opinion will arise about what was intended at the bargaining table or how the clause can be implemented in the daily work situation. Often the cause for dissention is that the subsequent situations were never anticipated and the question arises as to whether the existing language is appropriate or broad enough to handle the matter at issue. Preparing the labor-management agreement language is of course extremely important. To sum up: If the agreement is not written by the solicitor, it should be reviewed by him. The language must clearly express the intention of the negotiating parties. The language should be clear, concise, and as simple as possible. A decision must be made as to whether it should be couched in legal or shop language. The clauses, of course, should follow an orderly sequence. And lastly, it is most important that sections that are revised be free from ambiguity and not overlap on other new or existing clauses.

Role of the Public Relations Agency

One of the agencies that might reasonably be expected to contribute to, or become involved in, a program of management-employee activities is public relations. On this subject, however, I will only speak from my own experience in Philadelphia. The city has a labor-management program and it also has a large public relations staff, but the public relations department plays no role in the employee relations program. There are, of course, a number of reasons why this is so.

I believe the first reason is due, in part, to the difference between the ground rules of industry and government for handling labor-management relations. In theory, government employees cannot strike. Industry uses public relations to get its message across to its employees and the public in the event of a strike. Industry publicity appeals to the workers before negotiations to explain management's position and what it proposes. During a strike industry states its position hoping to convince one and all that management is being very fair in its handling of the disagreement. It is important to note that industrial management speaks as one unit. This is not true in government.

I presume the situation is not much different anywhere in the public service, but without too much difficulty, 30 reporters from different papers can be found any day in Philadelphia's city hall. They dig up stories and get them into print faster than the public relations staff can put them out. A good reporter will have quite a few sources that he can contact. All are considered "management." Let us take a quick rundown. In addition to the bargaining team itself, there is the chief executive, the chief administrative officer, members of the city council, members of the civil service commission, the personnel director, and yes, the staffs of all of these officials. No wonder almost any story the public relations people hand to the newspapers on employee relations is two days old and three newspapers late!

The second reason why government public relations people are at a disadvantage in writing about labor-management relations is that after management and the employee organization have come to an agreement, the members of the employee organization must meet and ratify that agreement, before any, I repeat any, publicity can be put out. The employees hold their meeting at night, with one or more newspaper reporters standing by. Who do you think scoops the story? Management or the newspaper reporters?

The city administration does believe that it is good publicity to summarize the total package of benefits given to its employees and, accordingly, the public relations staff carefully prepares a handout.

The final trouble is: The story is such a rehash of what has appeared daily that it winds up as an insignificant news item.

Role of the Departmental Personnel Officer

The over-all fields of operations of departmental personnel officers parallel, or should parallel, those of the personnel director. Such an officer is in reality the personnel director of a department, which many times is larger in terms of employees than that of the average sized municipality. Stated in another manner, the personnel functions and responsibilities in a line department are—with the normal exceptions of recruitment and selection, classification and pay, and over-all policy development—those of administering the various programs of the jurisdiction's personnel system.

One of the programs in which the departmental personnel officer can play a major role is that of management-employee relations. His value and effectiveness in this field will depend in large part upon his knowledge and understanding of the subject, his competence in handling grievances, and the degree to which his department head will delegate responsibility. Most department heads are more than willing to delegate employee relations activities to someone else, if they can but find on their staff the competent individual who can handle such an assignment. I think the personnel officer should be that person, and I think he has the responsibility to prepare himself to handle the task. These are the areas to which attention must be given, and the departmental personnel officer can reasonably expect to be involved in them for no less than 10 per cent of his working hours.

1. He must clearly know the jurisdiction's labor-management provisions and any related legislation affecting those provisions. (The employee organization representative will know them frontwards and backwards and management's representative had better be as well informed.)

2. He should be the official department interpreter of labor-management agreement clauses and, in doing so, should maintain liaison for top policy interpretations with the central personnel agency and/or the official spokesman on labor-management policy. As interpreter he will probably also have the task of training or instructing new supervisors on labor relations policies and in handling disciplinary problems. He must make sure that supervisors know their authority and understand the agreement requirements sufficiently to answer questions from employees. He must make sure that they have been trained to avoid making concessions either orally or through lax enforcement in settling day-to-day disputes.

3. He should be a kind of watchdog, assuring the maintenance of management's rights in the department in accordance with the terms of the labor-management agreement. More and more, management finds itself faced with "past practice violations" grievances. Innocent, innocuous, and what may appear to a supervisor to be a harmless concession—a deviation from established practices or management accommodation—these are practices and actions which may later come to haunt management. The departmental personnel officer must constantly be on his guard to prevent such whittling-away of management's established rights.

4. He should advise and/or recommend departmental rules and policies regarding labor-management practices. Because he is the focal point of all labor-management activities in his department he should become the expert adviser on new or revised rules for internal use in the agency.

5. Finally, he should handle and/or negotiate most of the grievances involving departmental employees. To ensure uniformity of administration of the grievance process, disciplinary investigations, and penalties, responsibility should be formally delegated for overall accountability. The departmental personnel officer may very well be delegated to develop—with the representatives of the employee organization—the grievance procedure, its steps, violations, and penalties. He may serve as chairman of the grievance committee, and depending on the regard with which he is held by his superior, may very well be given authority to act, subject to various appeals procedures. (As an indication that this can work, the Personnel Officer at our 2400 bed hospital last year settled all of the grievances at the first two steps of their grievance procedure at scheduled weekly grievance meetings. None reached the third step which involves the Hospital Superintendent.)

Conclusion

At the beginning of this discussion I said that because of the differences in the characteristics and the status of employee relations in each locality that insofar as possible my remarks would be of a generalized nature. While I have tried to adhere to that commitment, the subsections of my paper have required that I draw, in part, on my personal views and past experiences. And, of course, my experiences are not necessarily established patterns or in the context of any other person's employment situation. I hope I have not created a confused picture. Let me close by saying again that my intention has been to make suggestions which can be applied—by adaptation—to your jurisdiction.

9.

Organizing Management for Employee Relations

Douglas G. Weiford

The subject of management-employee relations in the public service is both fascinating and elusive. In the sense that it involves the emotional biases of the individual personality, I consider it quite impossible to offer precise and absolute solutions. As a matter of fact, at the present time it is difficult to find people who can agree on anything other than that the subject is one of great interest, that it is growing in importance, and that it lends itself to violent opposites of opinion.

The Problem Is Difficult

Assume, for example, that you come to me and ask: "How can we establish effective and workable employee relations in our local governments, large and small?" I reply: "I cannot give a satisfactory specific answer to your question." But you persist: "Given the drive by public employees to utilize union procedures heretofore found only in private industry, what can we do to develop sound and harmonious employee relations?" To this, I must reply: "It all depends! First you must tell me about your local government. In what state is it located? What is its size, its economic base, its social history, and its political composition? What kind of people are your current decision-makers? What are their personalities, their prejudices, their attitudes?" And you ask: "Is it really as difficult as all this?" And I reply: "It is not only as difficult as that; it is confused and uncertain as well."

It is an unfortunate fact that satisfactory answers to most of the questions raised about management-employee relations are not yet available. Relations with unions are becoming increasingly routine in the conduct of governmental affairs, but knowledge about public labor relations remains meager, full of many questions and few answers. It is a field which has now emerged as a formidable and extensive problem, but in which acceptable and workable definitions of the most basic terms are not available, and in which little consistency in policy exists from city to city and from state to state.

At the outset of my discussion of organizing management for employee relations I shall levy a blanket criticism of city officials. In recent years, we (I am a member of this group which I am judg-

90

ing) have devoted an enormous amount of time to the development
of knowledge about municipal affairs, to techniques and procedures,
to planning on the grand scale. I believe we have moved to meet
many new municipal problems with enthusiam and dedication. But
on this emerging business of labor relations, I believe that governmental officials have, thus far, done relatively little except talk—
and mostly in negative terms.

Steady Growth of Union Influence

In many of the cities and counties throughout the United States,
unionism of public employees is still relatively unknown. Terms
like "collective bargaining," "exclusive representation," "business
agent," and "deadlock" have a strange and unfamiliar ring. The
manner in which many local governments establish wage and fringe
benefit policies remains rather casual and largely unilateral. For
example, how many times have you seen a group of employees come
before the city council late in the budgetary process, stand politely
before the councilmen, file their requests, enter into a little discussion but no debate, and then depart. Sometime later, the council, in
the last-minute flurry of finishing their budgetary review, makes a
final and unilateral decision on wages and proceeds to some other
matter, perhaps more pressing, perhaps not.

The steady growth of unions in the public service indicates that
this casual approach to employee wage and fringe benefit matters
has about run its course. Whether municipal officials like it or not,
it must be recognized that employee organizations are steadily demanding and winning a bigger role than ever before in influencing
the official policies and practices that affect them.

Moreover, I think we can correctly assume that the future will
see a continued steady growth in the number of employee organizations, in the number of people holding membership in them, and in
the strength and influence that will be brought to bear on local government with respect to all matters affecting public personnel.

It is my own view that this trend, with all its inherent difficulties, is not entirely undesirable. For I believe that employee organizations and governmental management can frequently serve com-
plementary rather than antagonistic roles in accomplishing the purposes of government.

As most of you know, Wisconsin law requires the officials of
local governments to recognize unions and to bargain with them under "good faith" conditions. If a deadlock finally results, either
party to the dispute may petition the Wisconsin Employment Relations Board to institute advisory fact-finding procedures.

Among many local government officials this law has caused head shaking, murmurings of disaster, spirited discussion, and occasionally violent argument. But up to this point the sky has not fallen, and most objective observers would probably say that the law is working reasonably well. On one thing, though, all can reach agreement. The new Wisconsin law has radically changed the method by which local governments deal with their employees and has required public managers to give critical thought to the problem of reorganizing themselves to cope with this totally new concept of employee relationships.

Since there is reason to believe that some other states may follow Wisconsin's example, Wisconsin's experiences may offer guidance to those public managers who would be affected.

Throughout my presentation I shall convey my general approval of the trend toward formal negotiations between governments and their employees. At the same time, however, I will take care not to give the impression that all of this will take place in a kind of remote and peaceful Never-Never Land. By its very nature, labor relations is the stuff of which conflict is made. It is exhausting and tedious. It is full of emotionalism and political hazard. At times it develops into a hard, cruel business. And implicit in the whole process is conflict and struggle between traditional procedures and the goals of the various employee organizations.

Union Impact on Traditional
Personnel Practices

The growth of strong unions will interject into the daily routine of the public official substantial and sometimes startling changes. The financial impact is obvious. Cities that have not kept pace with advancing wages, changing working conditions, and modern personnel management will find aggressive union activity reflecting heavily on the municipal treasury. Perhaps even more important is the fact that various institutional procedures are certain to be challenged. Chief among these are the civil service system and the integrated pay plan. Indeed, the historic civil service system may be headed for a life and death struggle on the battlefield of collective bargaining.

So-called "merit" pay increases will come under bitter attack and, because they are based principally on hard-to-defend subjective standards, will often be replaced with across-the-board increases in each collective bargaining unit. The standard types of classification and pay plans will face frequent union onslaughts; annual attacks may be anticipated on pay ranges and classifications for various positions. Individual job holders on union advice can be expected to refuse work assignments unless the duties are set forth specifically in written job specifications. Joint management-union evaluation of job classifications will become common.

The diversified nature of municipal work encourages separate union organizations. Where a number of such unions exist they will be in competition with each other as well as with management. Each will struggle to better its position with the result that the traditional concept of "equal pay for equal work" on a government-wide basis and the maintenance of an over-all system of values in the classification plan will be increasingly difficult to maintain.

Aggressive unions will sometimes win concessions which are not awarded to nonorganized employees, resulting in problems of morale and the organization of additional bargaining units. Seniority rather than performance will be stressed as the principal criterion for promotion to nonsupervisory positions. Disciplinary problems will be carefully watched by unions, and members will be defended by union attorneys. Union membership will be considered by the individual worker in certain classes of position as more significant and more protective than civil service status.

Local governments will be required to spend considerable portions of each year both in direct negotiations and in time-consuming preliminary preparations. Struggles during negotiating sessions will become emotional at times, requiring formal procedures to minimize personal involvements on both sides of the bargaining table. As individuals, city councilmen can expect to receive pressures from unions both prior to, and during, negotiations. It should be anticipated that unions will often exert political pressures, including direct appeals to the public, for sympathy and support. When agreements are finally reached, they will increasingly be placed in contract form to be signed by both management and labor.

Even this brief recitation makes it perfectly obvious that the road ahead is not likely to provide smooth traveling. Nevertheless, the fact must be accepted that the formation of employee organizations flows from deep-seated human needs. Unions will continue to be formed and will grow stronger. All public officials elected and appointed must recognize this and develop the necessary attitudes and skills to cope with what lies ahead.

A number of provocative questions can be raised concerning the difficulties of incorporating formal labor relations techniques within the framework of government. Let us start with a very elementary but not simple-to-answer question. "Who constitutes management?" How can this be explained in categorical terms? The definition of "management" in Eau Claire, Wisconsin, for example, may be very different from that in a neighboring city. In general, those cities that have a so-called strong executive (either elected or appointed) will have a much easier task of answering the question. Those with a weak mayor form, with multitudes of boards and commissions, an independent civil service commission, and a scattering of elected administrative officials, may find this elementary question virtually unanswerable.

I submit that it is a healthy thing to be forced to think about our systems of government, procedures, and types of organization. I further submit that union activity is one of the forces of change that will require local governments to undertake some basic re-examination of elementary, but neglected, matters. Let me give you an example.

A certain city in Wisconsin with which I am familiar has never bothered to adopt formal personnel procedures. Systematic recruitment procedures and training methods have never been utilized. For years it has been the policy of this city to hire their laborers and semiskilled workers from the ranks of those who were either on relief or who were likely prospects for the relief rolls. Public employment in this city has thus been viewed as a kind of "dumping ground," and the standard of employee performance is about what you would expect under the circumstances.

When the Wisconsin Employment Relations Act was made applicable to municipal employees these refugees from the relief rolls formed a union and set about to bargain with the city council. Among other things, they demanded the same scale of wages that various other cities pay. They will probably succeed in achieving this goal. In a certain symbolic sense, the chickens have come home to roost. It may be half a generation before this city will be able to equate employee productivity with the wage levels it will be called on to pay.

Without any doubt, one of the most basic rules in organizing management for employee relations is the absolute necessity to establish and maintain recruitment and selection techniques of the highest quality.

Union Criticisms of Public Managers

Before discussing other elements in the organization of management for employee relations, let me digress for a moment.

In his excellent article, which appears as Chapter 4 in the Public Personnel Association's handbook on "Management Relations with Organized Public Employees," Eli Rock points out that many governmental officials view collective bargaining and other formal dealings with unions as an "evil art." The implication he draws is that labor relations in many cities are chaotic primarily because officials look at the entire process with dislike and misgiving.

Perhaps we would do well to realize that employee relations is a two-way street and that employee organizations judge us even as we judge them. We, too, can conduct ourselves in such a manner as to appear to others as being practitioners of an evil art. We, too, can organize ourselves (or fail to organize) in such a way as virtually to insure conflict and dissension.

I thought you might be interested in some complaints that unions have about public officials, so I asked the Executive Director of the Wisconsin Council of County and Municipal Employees about the pet peeves he and his field representatives encounter in dealing with local governments. His reply included these points:

"Grossly apparent in the collective bargaining relationships with the public employer is the complete lack of skill on the part of many public employers in bargaining with the union. There is an art to conducting negotiations. Over 90 per cent of the public employers have not mastered the basic fundamentals of the art.

"At the present time, city attorneys, district attorneys, city and county clerks, department heads and sundry other officials are all participating in bargaining. Continuity in the bargaining process is lacking and diversity of opinion is rampant.

"The public employer has a strong tendency to hold off bargaining until the final moments (budget time). A bargaining atmosphere produced by delay and procrastination is not good to say the least. Under these conditions the meetings with the union are too brief and too few. It is amazing how frustrated a union representative and the membership he represents can become whenever this happens.

"Another point is the fact that a great many public employers conduct a collective bargaining session as if it were a formal hearing. There is nothing, in my experience at least, that surpasses an informal gathering around a table as a device to bring off a successful bargaining session.

"There is a blind reluctance on the part of many public employers to accept a clause in an agreement providing for arbitration of any disputes that may arise from the agreement. It would seem to me that this is the only logical and reasonable method to use in settling unresolved disputes especially when we consider the alternatives.

"Finally, there are those important elements which fall under the head 'common courtesy.' We ask these things.

Please do not indulge in personalities. Answer correspondence and petitions promptly. Keep appointments and be on time. A union representative may have traveled a great distance to handle the bargaining, and the local officers may be sacrificing time and money to represent the union. Their business is just as important as yours. If the appointment is delayed or not kept, considerable money and effort are wasted and good will is impaired."

Negotiation Timetable in
Eau Claire, Wisconsin

With some of these comments in mind, I want to describe the still evolving method which we use in Eau Claire, Wisconsin, during the negotiating process.

The fiscal year in Eau Claire begins on January 1, and this means that the city council is heavily engaged in budget review and hearings in the fall—during the months of September, October, and November. The budget is customarily adopted and the tax rate fixed around December 1. Many local governments throughout the country follow this same procedure, but because of the new Wisconsin law one very important part of the Eau Claire budgetary process now starts in the spring. Active negotiations with employee organizations begin on July 6, and this means that it is necessary for us to begin assembling data needed in these bargaining sessions as early as May 1. In other words, the law caused the City of Eau Claire to establish a specific and orderly timetable for negotiations—a timetable which would presumably provide sufficient opportunity for bona fide bargaining and also time for advisory fact-finding procedures in the event of a deadlock, all in advance of the date on which the proposed budget and tax rate must be published.

The Eau Claire labor relations timetable sets aside the months of July and August for the bargaining process, and during this period a substantial number of negotiating sessions are conducted with each bargaining unit. It is always to be hoped that agreements will be worked out during these 60 days, and sometimes this will be the case, sometimes not. But regardless of the outcome, the processes of government must continue. Negotiations with employees on financial matters cannot proceed indefinitely. The budget must be adopted and the tax rate fixed; failure to reach agreement cannot stay these unmovable deadlines. Agreement or no, at the end of August the city council makes its final decisions on the matters under negotiation and incorporates them in a resolution of intent. If the union groups have not already agreed, and now determine that the council's final offer is unacceptable, state law provides that they may, at their discretion, utilize the months of September and October for advisory fact-finding.

The theory of this plan is that the city council is bound by accepted democratic processes to incorporate in their proposed budget, prior to the public hearing on the budget, all of their preliminary decisions relating to the expenditure of public funds for the forthcoming year. Only in this way can the public have the opportunity to express itself at the hearing before final action is taken on the proposed level of taxation.

Consequently, if a union declares that a deadlock exists, petitions the state for fact-finding, and obtains an advisory fact-finding, judgment within our 60-day period, the city council has the opportunity to consider the fact-finder's report in making their final decision.

Some students of municipal labor relations have stated that the bargaining process is not compatible with budget deadlines, and that city officials must reconcile themselves to what they call "open end" budgets. In other words, they believe (and fear) that settlements will not be reached until after the statutory date for the adoption of the budget has passed, and that funds for agreed-upon wages must be taken from a contingent account or diverted from some other planned program after the fiscal year has begun. Such action would, of course, increase the tax rate for subsequent years without public notice and hearing as normally required by statute.

In 1962 Eau Claire was involved in a fact finding case after the adoption of the budget and tax rate, and the city took the position that no deadlock could exist in such circumstances. In the words of one of the members of the Wisconsin Employment Relations Board

"The WERB has been presented with the question of whether a petition for fact-finding should be processed since the municipality's budgetary deadline had passed. The municipal employer argued that since the time for adopting the municipal budget had passed, no meaningful purpose could be served by fact-finding since no monies would be available to act upon the recommendations of the fact-finder. Therefore, the municipality did not have the capacity to negotiate further.

"The WERB rejected this argument, concluding that the municipality had the statutory authority to make changes with respect to the compensation and the number of positions in municipal employment if it felt that such changes were desirable. The WERB recognized that the municipal employer would not be obligated to make such changes, but that it could do so if it wanted to adopt the fact-finders' recommendations. The Board's memorandum stated that to adopt the argument of the municipal

97

employer would encourage municipalities to hide behind the shield of budget procedures to thwart the operation of collective bargaining, and would frustrate the legislative intent."

By the time this opinion was published, bargaining with the particular unit for a new year was already underway, and the city's position was not subjected to actual test. We were ready, however, to take the case to the Wisconsin Supreme Court on the grounds that the legislative intent in specifying that the public must receive notice and hearing prior to the adoption of a budget and tax rate is vital to a democratic society and supersedes any contrary demands of a small segment of the public, whether or not they are members of an employee bargaining unit.

In any event, the city determined that an orderly labor relations timetable was a suitable alternative and such was adopted. Whether the precise and orderly timetable will stand up under the pressures of actuality remains to be seen.

Negotiating Procedures in Strong Executive Cities

A city council surely is a most unlikely negotiating agency. It is by design a cumbersome thing, subject to all of the fierce and uncertain elements of political life. During something as delicate as labor negotiations it must be expected that each councilman will attempt to keep an eye on the attendant publicity, his personal image, the next election, and the tax rate all at the same time.

There is really nothing wrong with this. A typical city council is simply not a closely knit group in the manner of a private board of directors, and no one should want it any different. But this requires that we ask ourselves an almost unanswerable question: How is it possible to organize a city council for effective employee relations? Here again, we have no choice but to be pragmatic, for it is an inescapable fact that only the city council can make final decisions on financial matters. For this reason, it has been determined in Eau Claire that, difficult or not, the city council must perform an active role in labor negotiations.

In very large cities this decision may not be practical, and it will not be feasible in cities with grossly diffused managerial systems. In most council-manager cities, and in some mayor-council cities, it does, however, appear to offer possibilities. The various steps in the negotiation procedures are described below:

1. About two months prior to negotiations, start to assemble all necessary data. Study local wage rates for comparable municipal positions. Contact cities in the state of the same general size

and composition and pool information with them on wage rates and fringe benefits. Analyze the cost-of-living index. Develop this material in readable report form.

2. See to it that the unions file their requests at an early date. Develop the financial impact of their demands.

3. Submit all of this material to the city council.

4. Arrange for the full city council and the bargaining units to meet at least once and preferably twice in order to clarify all requests. Bargaining is not an academic process. If councilmen remain aloof and detached from the earthy process of battle, great trouble can lie ahead.

5. Once the atmosphere has been established and the demands and counterdemands clearly enunciated, the process can assume more flexibility and the chief executive (either mayor or manager), along with his staff and with a few designated council representatives can proceed with subsequent meetings on a more informal basis. In such a procedure the full council must receive detailed minutes of each meeting so as to remain in close touch with developments. If negotiations bog down, the full council may then re-enter the bargaining process and seek to find areas of agreement.

6. An air of informality is sought in all such meetings, and no business other than that of bargaining is ever scheduled. If agreements can be reached, well and good. But if all attempts fail, a final council decision is reached in late August and the details are placed in an official resolution.

7. Public employee unions will sometimes bring direct political pressure if the negotiation process does not give them what they want. Partly for that reason, and partly because of the public's right to be kept informed, all bargaining sessions in Eau Claire are public and are fully reported by newspapers and other news media. Deliberations (strategy sessions) of both parties take place in executive session, but the negotiations themselves are public. In our view this procedure facilitates the proper conduct of democratic government and at the same time provides some degree of protection from political attack if negotiations break down.

The Eau Claire Board of Education follows a somewhat similar procedure in bargaining with teachers and custodial employees. It is interesting to note that the board has bargained with its employees for at least 20 years and consequently was relatively unaffected by the adoption of the new law.

Negotiating Procedures in Diffused
Management Cities

Cities with diffused management, including independent civil service commissions, will very probably have a much more difficult task in developing an orderly labor relations procedure.

Many of our municipal organizations, for example, set the personnel director aside from the mainstream of management, so that he is neither fish nor fowl in this emerging area of labor relations. On this question I support the viewpoint that personnel administration is clearly a management function and that the concept of the independent personnel agency stands in need of re-examination.

At any rate, where managerial responsibility is scattered among a number of agencies and officials, there appears to be no alternative but to form a negotiating team representing all of the elements of management. Since such a team cannot make final decisions it can do no more than make recommendations on the matters under negotiation and hope for the best.

In this connection it seems clear that the emergence of strong unions in the public service will tend to make more urgent the need to re-evaluate those governmental structures and procedures which originated primarily for the purpose of coping with problems of another era and which now tend to make the decision-making processes of government unduly slow and cumbersome.

A Few Questions and Answers

There are a few important questions which I have raised—then answered on the basis of my own experience and observations. Someone else might have a different opinion.

What are the differences between dealing with a local union and a national union? The major difference, in my view, is the broader perspective and the professional approach introduced by the business agent of the national union. Contrary to the municipal stereotype on this question, I prefer dealing with the professional as opposed to local talent.

What about unorganized employees? In Eau Claire we have taken no steps to include these people in the bargaining process and do not intend to do so. All citizens have the right to petition the city council and this obviously includes nonunion employees. The point of difference is that the city council is not obligated to bargain with such individuals or groups, nor do they have the legal right to seek advisory fact-finding if the council refuses to accede to their demands. It is inescapable fact, however, that the bargaining groups

100

usually gain benefits for the unorganized workers whenever they gain something for themselves.

What about the problem of exclusive representation? Once again, we must be realists. The formation of employee organizations is strictly an employee matter in which management cannot interfere. Nevertheless it is perfectly evident that the bargaining process extended to a multitude of separate bargaining units could seriously damage the effectiveness of the municipal organization. If exclusive representation is the alternative, then I favor it.

What effect is union activity likely to have on integrated pay plans? I suspect the bargaining process will probably require that at least three separate and distinct pay plans be established, one for trades and labor employees, one for the uniformed services, and one for the remaining classes.

Is there any special kind of training which should be given to department heads and other key management people to help them deal more effectively with the labor relations problem? The responsibility for bargaining should not be diffused among various and sundry line officials, but should remain the responsibility of the chief executive and his staff and of the legislative body. Thus I do not consider it necessary to go beyond the routinely accepted principles of personnel administration in training the various management levels. Such training, however, must be consistently applied. Otherwise the embarrassing situation is likely to arise where the union leaders consistently exhibit a greater knowledge of the city's personnel rules and procedures than do some of the management people.

Some Conclusions

My own basic philosophy on unions in the public service centers around two points: (1) Government is obligated to grant to its own employees the right of self-organization. (2) The use of economic weapons by governmental workers should be prohibited.

Once these conclusions are made, others inevitably follow. If employees are to be allowed the right to form or join labor organizations, then it follows that some orderly procedure should be developed for the official recognition of such organizations. It also seems evident that an orderly procedure for negotiating with these groups must be developed within the peculiar limitations of the governmental process.

Finally, if the use of economic weapons by government employees is to be prohibited, then some kind of alternative machinery must be established to help resolve disputes. By its very nature such machinery must bring impartial third parties into the picture, but because the fixing of wages, hours, and conditions of employment is legislative in nature it is clear that all third party referees must be limited to advisory roles.

If these conclusions have any validity at all, it would appear desirable for the broad outline of the labor relations pattern to be established by state law. Home rule arguments notwithstanding, it is my belief that a state statute similar to that adopted by Wisconsin is preference to the aimless conflict and struggle which otherwise almost surely awaits the local governments throughout the nation.

10. Labor Crises and the Role of Management

Raymond F. Male

I am grateful for the opportunity to present a few observations about labor problems in the public service. My assignment was to discuss ways and means of dealing with a labor "crisis" in a public agency—and I shall assume that crisis means a strike or a threatened strike.

In more than twenty years of experience in government, most of it involved with personnel administration, and the past five years of it as a state commissioner of labor and industry, I have become increasingly concerned about two aspects of the ways in which public agencies deal with labor problems.

First, I am struck by the fact that after decades of increasingly effective development of most aspects of a "system" of public personnel administration, we are still, by and large, relatively inexperienced amateurs when it comes to dealing with "workers," "labor," "unions," and work stoppages in government.

Second, we continue what seems to me to be a wholly unrealistic mythology about so-called basic differences between labor-management relationships in the private and public sectors of our economy.

I assume it was purely coincidental, but this invitation to discuss these problems came at the very moment that I found myself very much involved in the practical application of these theories in the form of a "crisis" in New Jersey. I didn't need another crisis, but certainly it is timely and it illustrates perfectly the principal points I want to make:

1. Most employee relations crises ought not to occur.

2. Management must take the initiative for heading off labor crises.

3. It is unrealistic to have different ground rules for the behavior of public and private employees.

4. We need to develop a logical philosophy of employee relations for the public service.

Story of a Crisis

The crisis which I, as Commissioner of Labor and Industry of New Jersey, was expected to help solve was the threat to strike three of the nursing homes licenced by the state. This was not an idle threat; a strike date had been set by a local union of hospital workers.

Background for Trouble

In New Jersey, a few nursing homes may be for limited profit but most are private, nonprofit institutions set up to care for themselves.

Why should the state be concerned about a strike in these private institutions? To begin with, the state cannot ignore either the personal and social hardships or the hazards to health and life that might occur in the event of a strike. The state also must be concerned and take action for an economic reason. Around 95 per cent of the patients in New Jersey nursing homes are supported by federal, state, or county public assistance funds that are allotted for permanently, totally disabled people; the elderly who need assistance; and medically indigent people. How much the state agrees to pay these private institutions for each day of care of these patients determines, as I think everyone will agree, how much the institution will pay its workers. I am fairly certain that a check will show that in every state few public or private employees receive lower wages and have poorer working conditions than do nursing home employees.

A few years ago New York and New Jersey made surveys of working conditions, wages, and fringe benefits in nursing homes. It was found that a few people were actually being paid 58-1/2¢ per hour—gross before tax deductions—and many were getting 80¢ an hour. Most economists believe that in industrialized states like New York and New Jersey a minimum of $1.50 an hour is needed to keep body and soul together. Is it surprising that employees struggling in difficult jobs at less than a living wage eventually come to believe a strike notice is the only way to get action to redress their grievances?

I don't for one moment want to forget the welfare of the sick people in the nursing homes. But I submit to you that critical as it may be to head off a strike in a hospital, it may be more critical not to have that weapon available to workers to alert management, government, the customers of government, and the public that they must do something; that they cannot go on ignoring the problem.

For the moment, let us not argue the question of whether a strike is callous in a private hospital but an illegal act in a public hospital. Instead, let us try to answer this question honestly: "Which risks life more—a strike or the alternative—a year, or a decade, or a generation of the miserable kind of personnel practice that makes it impossible for the hospital to recruit and keep enough qualified nurses, attendants, orderlies, and other personnel to give decent basic care to sick people?"

Crisis Prevention Fails

I have said that most crises shouldn't happen so I would like to explain how I, and a lot of other people, tried many months ago to set in motion the changes that would have prevented the nursing home crisis.

It was recognized that government payments for nursing home care affected the ability of the home to pay salaries. Everyone, including the management of the homes, agreed that wages were shockingly low and that something ought to be done. After careful study and consultation, a formula was developed that was accepted by the nursing homes, the involved public agencies, the governor, and the union. The governor's budget contained a request for the money that it would take to raise those 80- and 90¢-an-hour wages to $1.25. This is not a fortune, but it was a pretty good increase for these workers.

But now the whole effort to head off a crisis failed. The legislature, in its wisdom—perhaps because it wanted to hold down budgets, avoid new taxes, make sure that it could tell voters it had kept a tight, economical, efficient ship—said: "No. That's one item we can cut."

Who Was To Blame?

After a year and a half of mediating—trying to do all those traditional things that are called good labor management relations—I was very tempted to say that the legislature caused the 1964 nursing home crisis, and they could jolly well take the blame for it. I even thought that when the press called and asked me "When are you going to do something to head off this strike?" that I would say "On October 12, 1962!"

That would have made me feel a little better, temporarily, but the fact of the matter was that those of us who had tried to improve the lot of the nursing home employees also had to accept some blame. We looked ahead, but we didn't look ahead far enough. We should have anticipated the possibility of legislative indifference or hostility or ignorance. All interested parties—the governor, the commissioner of institutions and agencies,[*] the budget director, the health commissioner, the nursing home association, the union—should have helped the department of welfare explain why the million or so dollars was so desperately needed. Why must a crisis occur before we can all agree on a solution? As tough as it sometimes looks, there are always solutions.

How the Crisis Was Met

Looking back now on that inevitable day when the strike weapon was surely ready to be used, it can be recorded that the strike was averted by the adoption of wage increases, the implementation of the formula previously unused for lack of funds, and the "finding" of the money by administrative transfers, with legislative budget office approval, from balances in other welfare accounts. The balances were a product of a healthier economy and a lightened case load in other categories of public assistance.

The Tradition of Different Rules

Human nature being what it is, crises will never disappear entirely. But management will continue to be handicapped in its crisis prevention and curative efforts until we develop a logical philosophy of management-employee relations for the public service. That means, I think, that we must get rid of a lot of notions about chain of command, legislative-executive responsibility, sovereignty, security—all of the old scare words—before we can act constructively instead of pushing the panic button every time there is a labor dispute in government.

I cannot offer a blueprint for public employee relations, but I think I can demonstrate that some of the traditional regulations and practices help bring on labor crises and interfere with their settlement.

Is it necessary to have two clauses in the New Jersey Constitution about collective bargaining—one for private industry; another for the public service?

Why shouldn't there be a Wagner Act for public employees? This bill, passed in the thirties, tried to meet the needs of the people who work in the private sector of our economy. It seems to me that the men and women who work for the State of New Jersey and

---

[*] This department licenses and inspects the homes and pays, through another administrative arm, for the care of the medically indigent.

those who work for the Standard Oil Company of New Jersey want the same thing—adequate, equitable rates of pay, good working conditions, a chance to advance, recognition of their worth.

And there is very little difference in the work they do. Both public and private managers try to lead employees so they perform efficiently their particular skills or knowledge. Both public and private employees carry out similar duties—typing, operating a machine, developing a budget, reading a gauge, writing a press release, driving a truck, and listening to a grievance.

It would be interesting to hear the real reasons why the legislature of the state of Wisconsin excluded state employees when it set up grievance and bargaining procedures for employees of local government.

The Settlement of Disputes

The New Jersey Department of Labor and Industry has, of course, a whole setup for conciliation, mediation, and ultimate arbitration for private industry. But let's talk a little about these activities in the public service for it is different there.

"Conciliation" and "mediation" are two interesting terms to define, and I'll give you a human-interest definition of them. We had a very excellent young mediator in New Jersey who was hired to do the same work for Oregon, except that there he got more money and the title of "conciliator." I hadn't thought there was any real difference between these words, but when I visited my friend in Oregon I found I was wrong.

A mediator is in the communication business. He's a runner. He goes in one room; he goes in the other. Hopefully, he eventually gets both parties all in the same room, with an agreement. A conciliator does a little less walking and practices a form of therapy. In other words, he doesn't wait for a consensus. He helps to create it. Now this is my own amateur definition, but I hope it shows that honest efforts to talk about problems usually will result in a mutually satisfactory settlement of differences. There are, however, people in the public service who still believe in management's prerogative to make a unilateral decision. They feel that somehow or other "they have been robbed" if they have to share decision making with employees or their representatives. This is the kind of attitude that brings on a demand for compulsory arbitration.

Now I am not going to advocate compulsory arbitration for the public service. I might have once, but I don't like to copy other people's mistakes! By law, most of the provinces in Canada have had compulsory arbitration. My Canadian friends tell me they are going to abandon it. Why? Because public management and public employees both sit back and do nothing about honest-to-goodness negotiation, knowing full well that ultimately time will run its course and somebody will come along with compulsory arbitration and work it out and neither management nor employees will look bad. So I accept Canada's rejection. It fits in with my own views about doing everything possible to prevent buck passing.

But what about advisory arbitration? That is often used in government. Sometimes one person is asked to make a suggestion, but more often an odd-numbered group is designated—for example, one person from labor, one person from management, and a third person who represents the public interest.

From my own experience, I would say that what usually happens is this. The labor man votes for the labor view; the management man for that of management; and the third man becomes, in fact, the arbiter. The decision is not binding, but there are not many public officials, elected or appointed, who quietly file an arbitration report even though it is advisory.

It is my view, therefore, that the most healthy situation seems to be when management and employee representatives are expected to settle their differences, but are aware of the possibility that their dispute will be turned over for consideration by outsiders. Usually this situation exerts a very salutary effect on their behavior.

A Realistic View of Strikes

Before the Governor of New Jersey appointed me Commissioner of Labor and Industry I had served as President of the New Jersey Civil Service Commission. I had already had experience dealing with both organized and unorganized employees, and I had learned, I think, how to tell whether some difference of opinion between management and employees was, or was not, at crisis. But it was here that I first heard arguments in favor of the right of public employees to strike. I learned them from Dr. William S. Carpenter, the conservative Princeton University professor who had preceded me in presiding over the Civil Service Commission of New Jersey. In a book called "The Unfinished Business of Civil Service Reform," the late Dr. Carpenter spelled out the reasons why he felt that it might be in the public interest even for firemen to have the right to strike. That still shocks me a bit, but I commend his reasoning to the attention of every public manager.

Most people have not shared Dr. Carpenter's point of view. Strikes by public employees have more often been described by such words as illegal, immoral, unconstitutional, unconscionable. But name calling has not eliminated striking. David Ziskind once counted up the number of strikes that had occurred between 1835 and 1945 and wrote a book called "One Thousand Strikes of Government Employees." (Actually, there 1,116.) I haven't seen any count for the past quarter of a century, but I know there have been a considerable number—except, of course, for those places that have "outlawed" strikes. A friend from New York state once explained this situation to me. He said: "When employees put pickets around city hall and all the other government buildings and nobody comes to work that's not a strike; that's a demonstration!" I think that a law like the Condon-Wadlin Act in New York State is an act of fright. The fact that it has been so little used seems to support that conclusion.

Oh, the cries of the wounded when somebody strikes against government. "Of the people, by the people, for the people. You can't strike against us. When you took this job, you understood that, didn't you?"

By what stretch of logic does a strike of elevator operators or charwomen or clerks employed by Central City represent a threat to sovereignty, whereas a strike of bus drivers employed by the Acme Transit Company of Central City must be protected by law? As a matter of hard, cold fact, the lack of transportation will have a more damaging effect on government and on the general public than the lack of someone to dust the mayor's desk at night.

How can we argue that a strike of employees of publicly owned ferry boats is illegal whereas the same kind of employees, operating the same kind of privately owned ferry boats, plying the same stretch of water, is legal and their rights collectively to refrain from working and collectively to bargain about their pay checks and other matters must be protected? And is it not an additional indignity to punish public employees when the whole purpose of a strike by private employees is to obtain a benefit?

No, it is not my intention to play a semantic ball game with the strikes-in-the-public-service-question (or to pun either). I don't go all the way with Dr. Carpenter's thesis that everybody has the right to strike. I think I can sum up my own attitudes in this way.

We must stop making like ostriches and come up with some realistic rules for dealing with strikes or demonstrations or economic sanctions or whatever we prefer to call them when they happen in government. Most public employees should have the right to strike. When it is determined that—for very clear and valid needs to protect the health, safety, or welfare of the public—certain employees must give up the right to strike there must be a quid pro quo. There must be a procedure to assure that a policeman, for example, gets a decent wage and suitable benefits; has proper weapons, up-to-date equipment, and adequate apparel. It is possible, I believe to justify and administer effectively a no-strike policy for a limited group of employees.

One of the reasons I lean in the direction of letting most public employees keep the strike weapon is that it stops buck passing. Right after World War II, I was personnel director of a New Jersey department that administered a hospital for the criminally insane. All during the war this hospital, like many others, had depended to a large extent on conscientious objectors to help them meet the need for attendants. Now the CO's had gone home and the remaining attendants were overworked and underpaid.

Before the Christmas Eve of 1945 when a strike was threatened, management had been passing the buck. I told questioning employees this: "What more can I do? I put in a request for pay increases, and it was not even approved in the budget." The Budget Director said: "The Director of Revenue tells me that the taxes just won't yield enough money for any pay increases. If we don't take it in, we can't spend it, you know." The Governor said: "I can only ask the Legislature. I can't make them appropriate the money." The legislators said: "The people just won't stand for a tax increase." On Christmas Eve, however, we made twenty years of progress in four hours. This is not a unique example of why employees cherish the right to strike. The effectiveness of striking, or a threat to strike, is demonstrated by the data reported by Ziskind in his book about strikes in the public service mentioned earlier. He found that 75 per cent of all of the public service strikes were settled within a week, 20 per cent within one day, and 10 per cent did not last for even a day.

A Realistic View of Unions

I do not have a crystal ball, but I think everyone will agree with me that the unionization of public employees is going to continue. Since this is so, we—read management—have got to learn to deal responsibly with union representatives.

I have seen friends of mine, public administrators at federal, state, and local levels, who have dealt in the most able and pleasant terms with other human beings until they found out that they were in the employ or were members of unions. Then they froze up. Before the awful truth was known, when the man met them in the corridor of city hall and said, "Sir, I would like to ask you about a problem," my friend would say "Come on in my office," or "Let's have a cup of coffee and talk about it." Afterwards he would say

"Let my secretary arrange an appointment." You see, that's the way to deal with union people.

I don't want to be facetious, but I think that if public managers search their experience they will agree with me that our group has tended to have a feeling of antipathy toward the union organizer and the union member. Somehow these people have frightened us. We have never learned to live with them or work with them, and because we haven't we get some unneeded crises.

In my opinion, the first thing for managers to do is to get acquainted with union people. When I was President of the New Jersey Civil Service Commission I spent a great deal of my time getting acquainted with representatives of organized employees and with their membership. I went to banquets and I went to picnics. I went because I was trying to understand what the organizations wanted and I was trying to explain to them the situation in which I was operating.

The second thing for managers to do is to approach union people properly. After many years of trying to apply this principle, I am convinced it is crucial for successful employee relations. It takes two to tango—or to tangle. If you want union men to fight you, be supercilious. If you want them to listen to your side of the story, listen to theirs. I know that sounds simple, but it is a simple truth.

A Word About Politics

"Politics" will be a major factor in every labor crisis between public employees and public management. Perhaps I use the word politics differently than some people do. I use it respectfully as a term of realism, as a term involving the interpersonal human relationships. Only if it is bad to be human is politics bad.

In every management-employee confrontation there will be a number of groups looking out for their own interests. There will be internal pressures by various members of management, union officials, and employee groups. Many external groups also will have an interest, a political interest if you will, in how things go in government—newspaper, church, professional organization, business association—you name it.

I think it is a real misfortune for democratic government that so many people are suspicious of activities like politics and lobbying. No stigma should, in principle, be attached to either practice. It is natural, legitimate, and even desirable for groups to try to influence a decision that will affect them. Consensus comes from a sifting and weighing of all available information and views. The public interest is sustained when courageous political leadership acts on such a consensus.

I have been around a long time, and I know that pressure groups often pervert their influence. But I believe there is a way to use their knowledge to advantage and to control their tendency to be selfish. The way is, as I said earlier, to develop a logical philosophy for public employee relations and to establish procedures for executing policy that are clear cut and easy to administer—or, as some say, to police.

A Word About the Merit System

Many people with long experience as public administrators sincerely believe that collective bargaining, mediation, and other methods of "sharing" decision making in the public service are illegal. They speak of legislative responsibility, sovereignty, and the rights of the public. They ask: "Why do we need a union? We have a merit system."

I can speak to this question. I have presided over a merit system. I know that the average public employee does not look to those of us who are civil service commissioners, merit system directors, or personnel administrators as being wholly their chosen representatives. Instead, we should recognize that it is membership in a union that provides for some employees, at least in their eyes, the possibility of choosing a representative who will bravely, intelligently, and articulately speak up for him to management in government. The union representative will not have divided loyalties.

Looking Ahead

I would like to make it clear as I end this discussion that it was not my intention to preach or editorialize. I don't believe I have all the answers. I don't know anyone who does. I am old enough, however, to believe that experience has some value.

I hope it is not inevitable that we have to go through the same birth pains of labor management relations that industry did. We ought to profit by their mistakes and successes. We ought to be able to profit from each other's experiences. The various governments in the United States differ greatly in the way they deal with employees. Let's discuss these differences frankly at meetings, read all the press clippings, books, and articles we can find. Fact finding followed by the courage to try out promising ways to solve problems is the way to develop a positive technique for conducting employee relations.

Let's stop mouthing words like sovereignty and right to excuse inaction. We need solutions. Let's stop being scared and illogical. Let's look with reality at labor management relations in the public service—as they have been—as they are—and as we want them to be in the months and in the years ahead.

11.

Adjusting to New Public Personnel Policies

Frank P. Zeidler

It is not an exaggeration to state that an important shift of political power in American government is showing up in the changing patterns of public personnel policies in the current scene.

These changing patterns, which reflect a stronger position of the public employee with respect to administrative officials and with elected legislative bodies, seem to stem from the increase in the number of public employees. The increase in public employees comes about as the result of greater public demands for government service. The greater demands for public service have occurred as a result of our changing technology. This changing technology has permitted a higher standard of living, but it has also left in its wake a host of welfare and social problems, of which chronic unemployment is not the least.

When private efforts did not find ways to solve many of the problems created by technology, there was a public demand that some agency of government be given the task. As a result, new governmental agencies have appeared, and the employment rolls of existing ones have swelled. With the increase in governmental employment, there has come about the inevitable tendency of numerous employees doing the same kind of work to organize for pay increases and additional benefits.

Employee organizations in the public service, like their counterparts in private enterprise, try to make the employer yield a higher return to the employee, and this is a legitimate objective in both cases. However, public employees where they are numerous and well organized, have strength to influence public managers not only by direct negotiation; they also influence public policy through legislative bodies. It seems evident from a review of recent personnel acts, that many legislative bodies have receded from their former positions of unquestioned authority to determine rates of compensation of public employees and conditions of work. This authority is being yielded to other groups, such as arbitration agencies, or is made subject to agreements reached by private employers, or contractors and their employees, as in the case of construction workers.

A shift is thus occurring in which the public, through its legislative bodies, has yielded a part of its authority to make decisions

114

on terms of employment. Whether this is right or wrong will be determined by experience only. The determination will take place in the degree to which the arbitrary authority of government to make decisions on employment is not assumed by employee organizations who try to force their own arbitrary decisions on a government and hence on the people.

Improvement in Management-Employee Relationships Is a Joint Responsibility

In a democracy public administrators and public employees have a special obligation. They are both the servants of the people, however much this sounds like a cliché. Administrators and the employees jointly owe it to the public and the taxpayers to keep their relationships in such a state that there is no breakdown in the public service. Finally, they both have an obligation to conduct the public business efficiently, economically, intelligently and courteously. The public, in turn, owes to both management and employees just, perhaps even generous, compensation with no undue sacrifice of health.

To achieve these objectives, good communications and good liaison must exist between public management and public employees. It is the duty of both of these elements of the public service to establish and maintain good relationships. If the rule of public management is to effectively manage the public service, it is a task of management to take the initiative in establishing employment policies and in helping establish effective management-employment relationships to carry out the public business. The initiative in creating these relationships should begin with management.

There are pressures in modern conditions which lay a responsibility on public management to create improved management-employee relationships. These pressures have their sources in the changing technology, in the growing population, and in the demands placed on natural resources, which require ever more sophisticated and effective management. Improved management-employee relationships are not only required for the protection and defense of management prerogatives, they are also needed simply to get the public business done better.

Public Administrators Need a Philosophy of Management

Management must develop a philosophy of public service if it is to play its role effectively. The philosophy on its part need not necessarily be new—perhaps only a restatement or reformulation of aims. Some of the ingredients of this philosophy might be as follows:

Public management practices must be consistent with the philosophy of democracy. There are some boundaries of rights of the public or public employees that management cannot overstep. We might restate this point by saying that the arbitrary bureaucratic procedures of a totalitarian government or military order cannot be applied in democratic government, even in the area of police services.

Public management must represent as nearly as possible the interest of the whole public, not just a segment of that public. Public management cannot yield to any kind of pressure group in the community. It cannot represent commercial interests, labor interests, or even the interests of powerful management bureaucracies. Instead, public management must try to represent all groups, preferably in perfect consonance with the legislative body which is above management.

Legislative bodies, the people, and public management must comprehend that the interests of the public do not require continual excessive sacrifices of the public employee above the sacrifices required by other segments of society, but that public employees at the same time are required to maintain high standards of performance. One example will illustrate this dictum. Police and fire departments should be required to maintain high group and individual standards, but local governments must expect to pay fire and police personnel enough to compensate for the extra demands on them.

Public management should recognize that the best cooperation from public employees comes largely as the expression of intelligent men and women who understand the goals and objectives of their work and who are satisfied through fair treatment and good working conditions. This does not imply that public management does not require, or need, at times the final authority to carry out a policy or get a job done. The best strength of management comes from selling the logic of its objectives and practices to intelligent and reasonable employees who can grasp the conditions under which public management is constrained to operate.

Public management should recognize that the public requires high individual qualities of leadership, conduct, and judgment in those selected as managers of the public business. This point is not usually forgotten by administrators, but the force of it is often not recognized by people who are not in managerial posts. The public manager operates under the critical gaze of the public.

In the new order of employee organization, public management should remember that whether one deals with informal groups or formal organizations, there remains a place in the public business for concern for the individual either in his role as a citizen or as an employee. The distinguishing mark between a democracy and other forms of government is the concern of government for the individual. He must not be lost in the mass. If this happens, democracy will die. Public administrators must be concerned with the individual and cannot let organized groups extinguish his voice.

Management must maintain its prerogatives of authority but temper justice with mercy.

Who Takes Initiative for Better Personnel Relationships?

Fortified by a philosophy of public management, public administrators must take cognizance of the fact that they need continually to learn new techniques of personnel administration. Changing technology and changing patterns of life compel changes in the way public service is rendered. New types of service must be rendered with new tools and new methods. New positions must be created and old ones changed. These conditions require public administrators to continually evaluate employees' work and to determine their qualifications and their training needs.

I believe progressive public administrators will recognize that they will have to possess a wide range of effective public personnel practices in order to cover all the kinds of employment conditions that will be found in various types of American communities. Improved public personnel practices must range from those needed for village government to those required by complex types of government such as that of New York City or the federal government. At each level more or less formal procedures must be developed if the relationships between management and employees are to be correct and effective.

In the more complicated governments, the initiative for formal employer-employee relationships probably will come from the employees. In the simpler levels of government, the public administrator must take the initiative in setting up proper relationships.

What Forces Compel Improved Personnel Practices?

As the numbers of people increase in America, the management of public affairs becomes more complicated. The more people there are, the more organizations and structures are required to deal with their problems. The number of organizations and administrative acts required to effect this management does not occur in a simple arithmetic ratio. I have never seen any mathematical study of this situation, but it seems to me that the number of organizations and administrative units tends to increase after a point in some geometric ratio.

There is a parallel to this idea in the per capita cost of local governments. After some point in population number, the lowest per capita cost is reached, and after that point the incremental cost per unit of population added becomes greater. It should be noted also that as the number of public personnel employees increases, the specialization of positions tends to grow. This naturally leads the employee to the idea of acting with others in his category as a unit to gain some objective in compensation or working conditions.

A third force to note is that the aggregation of many people in positions of like employment tends inevitably to create a common psychology and common outlook on their position among these employees and a common attitude toward their employer. Eventually this common view of their employer and his methods of operation tends to produce a common reaction toward his orders and wishes. Finally, this common reaction toward the employer by a group of employees tends to produce a common and united set of demands on the employer.

If the foregoing reasoning is true, then (1) there will be a certain critical number of persons in a given type of public employment; (2) these persons will tend to generate employee organizations—union or professional and (3) these organizations will present a set of demands on employers and force the formalizing of employer-employee relationships.

Many a public administrator, with his life already made too complicated by trying to meet the demands of factions in his governing council dreads the idea of employee organization and hopes that nobody will open up the subject. I believe the hope is futile. I have discovered from some years of public administration experience that the phenomenon tends to appear simply as a result of increased numbers of employees and of their specialization.

Differences Between Public and Private Employment

In improving relationships between public management and public employee groups, both employee and management people must recognize that there is not a complete similarity and parallelism between public and private management-employee relationships. In making this statement I am well aware that some unions claim that public employment is just like private employment.

I do not agree with this view. There are a number of areas in which there are important differences. The monopolistic character of some public services is one area of difference. The critical importance and essential nature of some public services for the public's health and survival is another. There are some kinds of public service that cannot be rendered by private agencies, such as police service. If any of these types of services failed, there would be serious public problems.

Another difference between public and private services is crucial—the right of the public to have full knowledge of its business, of what it is paying for services, of what demands are being made upon it by public employees, and of all the ramifications of any decision in personnel problems. Employee-employer relationships in the public service cannot be a private matter between the public managers and the employee representatives. Not only should the end results of the discussions between them be known; the discussions themselves must not be secret. The public must always insist that it has the right to know what goes in public personnel practices.

Basic Public Personnel Principles

When an organization starts to develop formal structures for public personnel practices, there are certain questions that need to be clarified or resolved.

The first question which needs to be asked and answered is: "Who constitutes management?" Is "management" the public administrator, a department head, an agency chief, a foreman on the job? Is management the elected body of representatives? If this question is not answered correctly, the public administrator, acting for an elected body, can be isolated in his personnel practices by an appeal over his head to the elected body which can be made to think that public administration is something apart from the governing body.

My own answer to this first basic question is this: The power of management resides in the people. This power is delegated to the elected body, which, in turn, may delegate it to certain public administrators. The public administrator then acts for the legislative body, and this delegation must not be forgotten by the legislative body when the administrator is dealing with public personnel processes.

When the above view is accepted and clearly remembered, the next question becomes more easy to resolve: "Who does the negotiating, bargaining, or administering for management—elected or appointed officials?" Again, in the last analysis, the elected representatives of the people are responsible. They, therefore, have the power to retain the negotiation process for themselves—as they do in some governments—or they can grant powers of administration or negotiation process to chief administrators who, in turn, can delegate some of their powers to subordinate officials. In any event, it should be clearly understood by everyone concerned who has what powers for what kind of personnel administration. Even in the smallest units of government this delegation of authority should be stated in formal terms to avoid misunderstandings. Some of the worst problems of employee-management relations that I have experienced have occurred in some local governments where everything was completely informal.

The reason that the locus of negotiating and administering power is important is illustrated in larger governments where strong employee organizations exist. In such situations when employee organizations are dissatisfied in the negotiating process, they will often insist on going beyond the delegated administrative officer engaged in the negotiation and will press their claims with the local legislative body. Failing there, they may go to the state legislature. If this process is resorted to too frequently, the legislative body might as well become the negotiating body at once.

This type of negotiating activity can conceivably diminish the ability of the legislative body to take care of other segments of the public business, and in the end injure the public, injure administrative efficiency, and reduce job opportunities in the public employment because it takes too much effort to get public programs under way.

The Role of Public Personnel Commissions

With the growth of employee organizations, a subtle change is occurring in the role of public personnel commissions, and this change is raising a very crucial question: What will be the role of civil service or other public personnel commissions in a new era of employer-employee relationships in the public service? The original role conceived for these commissions was to protect public employees on the job from arbitrary discharge or mistreatment by any politicians who were boodlers, grafters, or spoilsmen.

The commissions have done excellent work throughout the nation when one considers the tasks of recruiting, classification, extension of employee benefits, and establishment of grievance procedures. With the growth of employee organizations, however, personnel commissions are victims of a subtle change in the psychology of the employee who has the benefit of civil service. The employee begins to regard his public employer much in the same way a private employee regards his employer, namely as one who seeks to exploit him as much as possible—in the case of public employment in order to keep the tax rate down. The employer becomes a kind of enemy with whom to do battle, and the public personnel commission in his mind becomes a tool and agency of public management. When this happens the employee no longer looks to the personnel commission for protection but turns to his union for help.

This new attitude among employees leaves personnel commissioners with a kind of frustration. They usually conceive themselves as persons having the highest welfare of the public employee in mind, and they are taken aback by the new conception of themselves in the minds of many employees. Many employees do not want what they regard as the paternalism of public personnel commissioners.

I think it will be a mistake if public personnel commissions retreat from the original concept of employee protection and the regularization of employee management relations. Personnel commissions, of course, will need to expand their ability to supply public administration officials with information and staff services in the matters of management-employee relations; but they will also be needed in the customary work such personnel commissions perform in classification, position determination, grievance procedure, and administration of employee benefits.

Public Management Attitudes Toward Employee Organizations

A question that definitely needs a clear answer is this: "What is the attitude of management toward the organization of public employees?" This question requires more thought than has heretofore been given it, but I do not think there is any easy answer. The traditional opposition to employee organization per se is a thing of the past, but the question of the propriety or legality of a particular formal organization is a matter not yet resolved. The type and kind of organization set up by police officers, for example, and the powers claimed for members in matters that could affect the public interest would have a crucial effect on the attitude of public managers toward the organization.

There is, it seems to me, one issue that must be considered "settled" in this still nebulous area of public management and official attitude of elected public officials toward employee organizations. This issue is the right to strike. In a democracy, with a truly representative government in office, it cannot be a prerogative of an employee organization to force a government to capitulate by striking a crucial service. If a strike can force a duly constituted, elected, democratic government to capitulate, this action signifies that the power of government has shifted from the people to employee organizations. A public employee organization cannot argue that it more fundamentally represents the people's interest than does a duly elected, representative, democratic government, and that therefore it can strike that government.

Spokesmen for some of the larger employee groups step gingerly around this issue and will not agree that they cannot strike. I believe there will be future tests of this issue as time passes.

Public Management and the Individual Employee

Still another, and vitally important, question to be resolved in public management-employee relationships is the attitude of democratic government toward the individual employee. Where public employee organizations are large and where the leadership is dominant with respect to the management, there will be a tendency to regard the individual voice of any employee as an intrusion on the prerogatives of the employee organization. It is at this point that a fundamental difference arises between the concept of public employment. In private employment the individual's statement, grievance, or protest can be suppressed or ignored by management. If the grievance, protest, or complaint of the individual cannot make itself heard through the employee organization, it need not be heard or considered at all.

In public employment, every individual employee who wants to be heard by government must be heard. He has a "right to petition government." The individual citizen also has the "right to be heard" on matters of public personnel policy and management-employee relations. It is absolutely vital to democracy that governing bodies provide in the management-employee relationship process some time for the hearing and considering of the statements, positions, and petitions of individuals. Whatever weight the governing bodies and public administrators want to give these individuals can be determined by their own judgment with regard to fairness. Naturally, unless these views are cogently put, they will not have the same weight as do the views expressed by groups, but it is an obligation of government to hear them.

Management Aids to Employees

Another question needing clarification and resolution can be posed as follows: "Should public management help unorganized employees formulate their requests, present their needs, or reflect their views?" The answer to this question appears to be that it is in the interest of management to provide opportunities and formal methods for employees, both organized and unorganized, to present their views on management policies. In this way, management gets a feedback on the effectiveness of its policies and actions. This

122

feedback is necessary for good management.

In improved public management-employee relationships, the question will arise as to whether or not management should advance claims for employees which the employees do not advance themselves. Put in another way, this question might read: "Should public administrators ask public elected officials for improved employee compensation when the employees do not advance such claims themselves?"

In my opinion, this type of action will frequently be required of public management for the protection of efficient public service. Many governments lose vitally needed public employees because of their unsatisfactory levels of compensation. Employees, such as physicians or engineers, are too few to organize for themselves or too weak politically to press their claims. Sometimes public managers have to press the claims for these categories of employees.

This kind of situation demands that public management fortify itself with facts and data on employee developments and practices, not only to defend itself against employee organization demands which are, or may be, unwarranted but also to meet needs which employee organizations overlook or are unaware of themselves.

Governmental-Union Relationships

In those places where elected bodies and public administrators recognize and deal with employee unions, the whole field of public management-employee relationships is entering into a period of much change. Informal procedures will no longer suffice, and many legal questions requiring nicety of solution will be confronting management and the employee unions alike.

Here are some of the types of questions which need answering in these circumstances, followed by the answer I would make if asked.

1. Is government-union bargaining equivalent to private bargaining?

My answer is that experience will show that it is not for reasons I stated above under the head "Differences Between Public and Private Employment." There are similarities, but they are not exactly equivalent.

2. Can bargaining and negotiating be kept to statutory and budget deadlines?

I believe that in the future bargaining and negotiating processes will not be kept within statutory and budget deadlines but will go on around the clock. Legislation will probably have to be enacted to meet this situation. Employee organizations resent the arbitrary shut-off of discussion, and they will undoubtedly seek to extend the negotiating process, by one device or another, beyond such deadlines. This condition will bring a new uncertainty into budgeting. The budget will never be wrapped up completely. If the budget deadlines are not adhered to, then one can expect the negotiating may go on for a long time, as it does in private management-employee relations.

3. Will arbitration be advocated with increasing insistency in all levels of government that recognize employee unions?

If the delegate public administrators deny an employee organization request or demand, the organization will naturally turn to the legislative body to overrule the public administrators. They do this now. If the public body turns down the request, the employee organizations will demand arbitration. At levels below the level of state government, I believe there will be a tendency to resort more frequently to arbitration when the local governing body turns down a request. This will occur because legislatures in some places will yield to the demand of organized employees to force local governments into arbitration.

4. If arbitration is accepted, do local governments lose some of their home rule powers?

Home rule is an historic demand of local governments. I think that arbitration is a diminution of the powers of home rule.

5. Is the state legislature likely to make more of the final decisions about local public management-employee relationships?

The tendency of organized employees to proceed to legislatures to get demands satisfied may be increased. However, this tendency is nothing new. Historically, local governments and state legislatures have struggled with each other over the tendency of legislatures to legislate on matters of public employment and compensation in local governments.

For this problem I have only two pieces of advice. If the legislature determines the rate of compensation for local employment, local governments should insist that the legislature also provide the revenue to pay for the salaries it prescribes. If the legislature insists that local governments have their decisions subject to arbitration, then those state employees who are under the legislature should have the same right to ask for arbitration when their demands are not met. This will enable the legislature to gain experience in what such arbitration means!

6. Who shall bargain and negotiate?

When a government recognizes employee organizations and agrees to bargain and negotiate, clear policies should be worked out between appointed and elected officials. Absent clear policies, the public administrator is liable to find himself negotiating without the support of the elected official. His own position will become untenable if he is overridden and made to look as if he erred either in assuming authority to bargain or with respect to the terms negotiated with employees.

7. What procedures are needed where the right to strike is clearly forbidden?

In the case of federal agencies, formal relationships should be set up with employee organizations, beyond those envisioned in President Kennedy's Executive Order 10988 for the purpose of obtaining continuous communication between federal employees and federal management officials. I believe there is value in establishing continuous formal management-employee sessions to prevent deep rifts from being established between management and employees and to catch grievances at their beginning when they might more readily be resolved.

8. What organizations are to be recognized, when, and under what conditions?

Recognition of employee organizations brings to government a host of problems. Competition between employee organizations has to be resolved and so do many kinds of intricate negotiating procedures. In this kind of detail, I predict that an enormous literature will develop to record the history of how these situations are resolved.

The Task Ahead

In the new and improved type of management-employee relations in the public service, the task of keeping the public informed is as formidable a one as any. It is the duty of public management to inform the public. Public information is necessary for intelligent public action. Public information is also needed to keep the public elected body properly supported by the people.

The public information process should not be used either by public management or public employee organizations as a method of waging warfare on each other. Such a technique is successful only for a short time; ultimately it becomes self-defeating. The public soon mistrusts anyone who looks like a manipulator.

The public personnel administration process will require greater competence on the part of the public administrator. He will have to fortify himself first of all by keeping informed about the latest techniques of administration. In addition, he must continuously collect data on administrative practices, on legal decisions that affect personnel practices, on employee organization activities and objectives, and on public attitudes concerning the kind and quality of services wanted and the level of taxes they consider acceptable.

How is the administrator to do all this? He must return to school. Sometimes the administrator can find advanced seminars in public service, including personnel policies in a university or college in his neighborhood. Sometimes he can attend local, state, or regional seminars. Mostly he must read the literature in his field.

In the matter of education, the Public Personnel Association and similar organizations can serve as centers where information is gathered and disseminated. These organizations need personal as well as financial support from public administrators.

The proper guidance and control of employees is vital to the success of any government program. The recruitment, testing, and selection of employees and the determination of their compensation must approach the surety of a science, although there will always be some art in public personnel administration. Organizations such as the Public Personnel Association, universities, and research organizations should be encouraged in their studies of personnel practices in order to keep practices modern and equal to the stress and strain of government operations. As in the exact sciences, so in this type of social science there is vital need for research and development.

Conclusion

In this paper I have endeavored to give the general boundaries and parameters of the new relationships between public management and public employees, both for organized and unorganized employees. Many problems that trouble the public administrator can be resolved within the framework of the ideas I have expressed.

I realize, however, that there are some more specific problems and situations that trouble administrators. Some of these problems are:

1. What bargaining units does one recognize?

2. Under what circumstances can a group withdraw from a union and be recognized as a separate bargaining unit?

3. What does the public manager do about unions whose members are hostile to their own elected bargaining representatives?

4. What does one do about unions who try to "out-compete" each other in getting agreements from the public administrator?

5. At what level does management stop and employee status begin?

6. What should be done about the demand of Negro organizations for special treatment in order to have more Negroes in the public service?

It is my opinion that the answers to each of these questions should be arrived at through bargaining and negotiation. Public management should review and study the problems that create these questions and decide which policy with respect to each it wants to follow. It must present its requests, demands, or what have you on public employee organizations as to the kind of procedure it needs to manage the public business.

It is not up to public management to get itself involved either in inter-union struggles for leadership, or intra-union struggles for membership. Management's task is to determine, with legislative backing, the conditions under which it will recognize employee organizations and how it will negotiate with them.

If the public administrator does not readily see the answer to certain knotty, specific problems, he has recourse to the Public Personnel Association and its host of contacts. Problems are seldom isolated or absolutely unique. Usually someone else has run into them before and found some kind of a solution. The public administrator must learn what his resources for help are in new situations. This point cannot be emphasized too strongly.

If what I have said here sounds formidable to the overworked public administrator, let me venture the opinion that the task of creating good public management-employee relations is formidable. It can only be satisfactorily met by the public administrator if he remembers fundamentally that he must act for the people and in the best interests of the people. If the administrator keeps this principle in mind, issues that seem hard or are open to expedient solutions will readily resolve into practical policies that put the administrator in a tenable and defensible position.

12. Legal Aspects of Collective Bargaining in Public Employment

Arvid Anderson

The past decade, and particularly the last five years, has been a period of rapid development in collective bargaining in public employment. The tremendous increase in the number of public employees is one of the factors contributing to the extension of collective bargaining in public employment. In 1960 there were 8.5 million employees in over 100,000 governmental units. Over 50 per cent were employed in local governments, 16 per cent in state governments, and 34 per cent by the federal government. (1)* Nearly one million public employees belong to a labor organization. (2)

For more than a quarter of a century, it has been the policy of the federal government and most state governments, by statutes and administrative programs, to encourage, promote, and protect the development of collective bargaining in private employment. Only recently has there been a similar trend in the public sector. The basic argument for the new encouragement of collective bargaining in public employment has been summarized as follows:

"A government which imposes upon private employers certain obligations in dealing with their employees may not in good faith refuse to deal with its own public servants on a reasonably similar basis, modified of course to meet the exigencies of public service." (3)

Federal Executive Order 10988

The most significant development of this period with respect to federal employees has been the Executive Order Number 10988 issued by President Kennedy on June 17, 1962, and supplemented on May 21, 1963 by the Presidential Memorandum, "Standards of Conduct for Employee Organizations and Code of Fair Labor Practices." (4)

Under terms of the Executive Order, employees are granted the right to form, join, and assist any employee organization or to refrain from such activity. Employee organizations may be granted any one of three kinds of recognition:

*All footnotes and citations are consolidated at the end of this paper.

128

1. "Informal" recognition means the right to be heard on matters of interest to its members, but management is under no obligation to seek the views of the organization;

2. "Formal" recognition means the organization represents 10 per cent or more of the employees in the unit. The organization has the right to speak for members, but may not speak for nonmembers and management must seek the views of the organization;

3. "Exclusive" recognition means the organization represents a majority of the employees and speaks for all of the employees in the appropriate unit. Management must confer and negotiate with the organization and can enter formal contracts affecting working conditions.

Management Rights Declared

The Executive order spells out a strong management rights declaration:

"Management officials of the agency retain the right, in accordance with applicable laws and regulations, (a) to direct employees of the agency, (b) to hire, promote, transfer, assign, and retain employees with the agency, and to suspend, demote, discharge, or take other disciplinary action against employees, (c) to relieve employees from duties because of lack of work or for other legitimate reasons, (d) to maintain the efficiency of the government operations entrusted to them, (3) to determine the methods, means and personnel by which such operations are to be conducted and (f) to take whatever actions may be necessary to carry out the mission of the agency in situations of emergency."

An appeal procedure for employee grievances was also established by Executive Order Number 10987.

Advisory arbitration is provided for bargaining unit determinations and to determine majority status. As of January 1, 1964, federal agencies were authorized to check off union dues pursuant to voluntary authorizations. (5)

Developments in the States

The federal program will undoubtedly influence the development of programs at the state and local level, both by the issuance of executive orders and by the enactment of statutes and ordinances. A number of state legislatures have adopted statutes encouraging employee organization and collective bargaining, while a few states have passed legislation designed to discourage such activity. Developments in 29 of the states are summarized below, followed by a detailed account of the Wisconsin program.

Alabama

In 1953, Alabama enacted a statute (the Solomon Act) which declares it to be the public policy of the state to discourage membership by state employees in a labor organization and subjects public employees who form or join a labor union to forfeiture of rights under the state merit system. The statute does, however, except city and county employees and teachers from its provisions. (Similar restrictions have been enacted by Arkansas, Georgia, North Carolina and Virginia.) (6) Alabama's Supreme Court has recently held that a public employer cannot contract with a union in the absence of express statutory or constitutional authority to do so. (7)

Alaska

A 1959 Alaska statute authorizes, but does not require, any political subdivision thereof to enter into union contracts with labor organizations representing public employees covering grievances, terms, or conditions of employment. (8)

Arkansas

In results that must seem ironic to its sponsors, "right-to-work" amendments to the Arkansas state constitution were the basis for invalidating a statute prohibiting policemen from belonging to a union. (9) The basis of the Arkansas decision was that, under the constitution, employees can join or refuse to join a labor union.

California

California has declared that public employees have the right to form, join, and participate in the activities of employee organizations of their own choosing for the purpose of representation on all matters pertaining to employer-employee relations, except as otherwise provided by law. Employees also have the right to refrain from such activities. Public employers are directed to meet and confer with employee organizations upon request and consider as fully as it deems reasonable the proposals of the employee organizations. A special statute with similar rights applies to firemen, but expressly prohibits strikes. (10)

Colorado

The absence of a Colorado statute led the Supreme Court of that

state to hold that a suit by a fireman to enforce a collective bargaining agreement with the City of Pueblo was not enforceable because the legislature, under the "home rule charter," could not delegate away by contract its duty to fix the terms of employment. (11)

Connecticut

A 1963 Connecticut statute confers upon local units of government the authority to bargain collectively with all employees except
teachers. The services of the state mediation board are made available to assist local units of government. The statute also appointed
a study commission to consider questions covering collective bargaining by municipalities, such as appropriate units; written agreements; and responsibility of municipal officials and employee organizations in bargaining, election procedures, and other relevant factors.

The commission is to report its recommendations to the Governor and legislature by January 15, 1965. (12) The exemption of
teachers from the statute is significant in that the Connecticut Supreme Court had determined in the landmark Norwalk Teachers'
Association case that teachers had the right to organize for the purposes of bargaining but not for the right to strike. (13)

Florida

A Florida statute which prohibits strikes by public employees
also confers upon such employees the right to join labor organizations and to present proposals relative to salaries and other conditions of employment through representatives of their own choosing
without coercion from their employer. (14)

Idaho

An Attorney General's opinion in the state of Idaho has held
that a municipality may enter into collective bargaining agreements
with its employees, provided no local ordinance forbids it. (15)

Illinois

In Illinois, the Chicago Transit Authority has been empowered
to enter into collective bargaining agreements with its employees.
The statute also provides that in the event of disputes over wages,
salaries, hours, working conditions, pension, or retirement provisions, such disputes may be submitted to arbitration. (16)

131

Iowa

Attorney General opinions in the state of Iowa have held that state employees may organize and join a labor union, but that the state does not have to recognize the union for bargaining purposes; nor may it be forced or coerced into doing so. The same opinion also held that the state has no authority to enter into union contracts. (17)

Maine

The Attorney General of Maine has given the opinion that deductions of union dues that have been authorized by the state or local unit of government for public employees does not confer the right of collective bargaining or arbitration. (18)

Maryland

The Maryland legislature authorized the Metropolitan Transit Authority to engage in collective bargaining with its employees and provided for arbitration of disputes over wages, hours, and conditions of employment. (19) But a Maryland Supreme Court holding has declared that a closed shop contract between a municipal employer and a labor union was unlawful. (20)

Massachusetts

Massachusetts enacted a statute in 1960 empowering any city or town, on a home-rule option basis, to engage in collective bargaining and to enter into collective bargaining agreements. The statute did not apply to police officers, probably reminiscent of the Boston Police strike. (21)

Michigan

The new constitution of the state of Michigan, which became effective on January 1, 1964, provides that the legislature may enact laws providing for the resolution of disputes covering public employees except those in the classified civil service. (22) Michigan's Hutchinson Act prohibits strikes by public employees and provides for the mediation of grievances in public employment and for fact-finding, with advisory recommendations for settlement in the event the municipal employer, by its governing body, agrees to such procedure. (23)

Minnesota

A Minnesota statute, which also prohibits public employee strikes, establishes the right of public employees to join or not to join labor organizations and to choose their own representatives. The statute authorizes the state Labor Conciliator to certify representatives, but a Minnesota Supreme Court ruling has seriously impaired the effectiveness of this procedure by holding that the Labor Conciliator is without authority to determine the appropriate bargaining unit in which the election is to be held. (24) Thus, unless the parties can agree on the collective bargaining unit, an election cannot be held.

Missouri

The Missouri Supreme Court has ruled that the state constitution, which grants the right to employees to organize and to bargain collectively through representatives of their own choosing, does not apply to public employees. (25)

Montana

The Montana Supreme Court held that a local school board was not authorized by the legislature to enter into a contract which gave a higher salary contract to union teachers than to nonunion teachers. (26)

New Hampshire

A 1963 New Hampshire statute authorized transit authorities created by cities and towns to contract with labor unions. (27) A 1957 decision of the New Hampshire Supreme Court has ruled that teachers could bargain collectively but did not have the right to strike. (28)

New Jersey

The constitution of New Jersey provides that public employees shall have the right to organize and to present to the state, or any of its political subdivisions, their grievances and proposals through representatives of their own choosing. (29)

New Mexico

An Attorney General's opinion in the state of New Mexico has stated that public employees can belong informally to unions, but they cannot engage in collective bargaining, picket, or strike against the government. (30)

New York

New York, by its constitution, confers upon employees the right to organize and to bargain collectively through representatives of their own choosing; however, a 1955 state court decision found that the constitutional provision did not impose a correlative duty to bargain collectively on public employers. (31) A 1963 statute required local units of government employing 100 or more full-time employees, except New York City, to establish grievance procedures consistent with the state statute by November 1, 1963. Grievances mean any claimed violation of law, regulations, or work rules that relate to health, safety, physical facilities, materials, equipment, or supervision. Grievances do not include wages or disciplinary proceedings which are otherwise covered by law. (32)

In 1963, the New York legislature amended the Condon-Wadlin Act of 1947 which bans public employee strikes. The amendment provides that employees who strike may not receive salary increases for six months (instead of for three years), will be on probation without tenure for one year (instead of five years), and will suffer a mandatory salary deduction equal to twice their daily compensation for each day they are on strike. The amendments are to be effective only until July 1, 1965, at which time their effectiveness will be evaluated by a study committee appointed by the Governor to make recommendations for possible future legislation on the over-all relationships between state and local governments and their employees. (33) In New York City, the Mayor's Executive Order on City Employee Relations has established collective bargaining for public employees. Similar action has been taken by the New York City Board of Education. (34)

North Carolina

North Carolina has expressly prohibited its public employees, state or local, from belonging to a national or international union and also declared that collective bargaining agreements between a municipality and any labor organization are void as against public policy. (35)

Ohio

The laws of the state of Ohio prohibit strikes by public employees upon penalty of termination of employment and loss of other employee rights. (36) Ohio statutes also permit publicly-owned utilities,

under a grandfather clause, to continue to contract with labor unions, if they previously had done so when privately owned. (37)

Oregon

The 1963 Oregon legislature has adopted a public employee
code which grants to employees of the state and its political subdivisions the right to form, join, and participate in the activities of
labor organizations of their own choosing for the purpose of representation and collective bargaining with their public employer. Public employers are prohibited from interfering, restraining, coercing, or discriminating against public employees in the exercise of
their right to organize and to bargain collectively. Public employers have the right to enter into collective bargaining agreements.
The mediation service of the state is authorized to aid the parties
in reaching an agreement. Strikes and picketing are expressly prohibited. (38)

Pennsylvania

Pennsylvania law prohibits strikes by public employees but
provides for the adjustment of grievances over working conditions
by a three-member panel. The Pennsylvania Supreme Court has
held that such procedure is applicable to disputes over wages and
that, therefore, the city of Pittsburgh was obligated to appoint its
member to the panel to discuss the firemen's demand for a wage
formula tying wages of firemen to other city employees. (39) In a
recent case the Pennsylvania courts have upheld the duty of a municipal employer under the above statute to arbitrate a seniority
grievance. (40)

Rhode Island

Rhode Island statutes permit state employees to organize and
join labor unions free from employer interference. Representatives
of state employees may present their views on grievances and conditions of employment which are not covered by the merit system.
(41) A 1961 statute gave firemen the right of self-organization,
representation, and the right to bargain collectively, provided they
do not strike. Compulsory arbitration is substituted as an alternative for establishing contract terms. A 1963 statute, which is very
similar, applies to policemen. (42) In 1958, state's highest court
held that teachers could bargain collectively but that they could
not strike in support of their demands. (43)

South Dakota

The "right-to-work" provision of the South Dakota constitution was the basis for that state's Supreme Court holding that a municipal regulation banning union membership by employees of its police, fire, and health departments was invalid. (44)

Texas

Texas now declares it to be against the public policy of the state and its political subdivisions to bargain collectively over conditions of employment, and strikes by public employees are prohibited. Nevertheless, Texas courts have upheld the right of labor organizations to represent public employees in the presentation of grievances and have upset city ordinances banning union membership by public employees as violations of the "right-to-work" amendment to the state constitution. (45)

Washington

The 1963 Washington legislature extended the right of collec-, tive bargaining to employees of publicly-owned utilities. (46) An Attorney General's opinion in that state has recognized the authority of county commissioners to enter into collective bargaining agreements including a union shop contract. (47)

The Wisconsin Program

In Wisconsin, legislative enactments tied in with administrative machinery provide a rather well-structured framework within which municipal employees and their employers are authorized to carry on joint relations on an organized, systematic basis. Because of the comprehensive nature of this program, it is discussed in some detail.

The Wisconsin statute, Section 111.70, enacted in 1959 and amended in 1962, grants to municipal employees 1) the right to join labor organizations; 2) the right to be represented by such labor organizations in conferences and negotiations with their municipal employers or their representatives on questions of wages, hours, and conditions of employment; and 3) the right to refrain from any and all such activities. The statute does not apply to employees of the state government.

The statute prohibits municipal employees from interfering with, restraining, or coercing any municipal employee in exercising the rights granted by the statute, and also prohibits the munici-

136

pal employer from encouraging or discouraging membership in a labor organization by discrimination in regard to hiring, tenure, or other terms or conditions of employment. Likewise, municipal employers are prohibited from coercing, intimidating, or interfering with municipal employees in the enjoyment of their legal rights, or from attempting to induce municipal employers to interfere with the rights of the employee.

Municipal employers are defined as any city, county, village, town, metropolitan sewage district, school district, or any other political subdivision of the state. Municipal employees are defined to include any employee of the municipal employer except city and village policemen, sheriff deputies, and county traffic officers. The latter group, however, does have a right to fact-finding whenever a majority of the members of a police, sheriff, or county traffic officer department petitions the governing body for changes or improvements in their wages, hours, or working conditions, and designates a representative which may be one of the petitioners or otherwise.

The Wisconsin Employment Relations Board

The 1962 amendment authorizes the Wisconsin Employment Relations Board to administer the statute, including enforcement of the prohibited practices section, and to determine questions of representation upon the petition of either the union or the municipal employer. Final orders of the Board are subject to judicial review.

The Wisconsin Employment Relations Board (referred to hereafter as "WERB") is also authorized to make its mediation services available to municipal employers and labor organizations upon their request. The statute provides for fact-finding with public recommendations in the event that the parties are deadlocked in negotiations, or where either party has failed or refused to meet and negotiate in good faith at reasonable times in a bona fide effort to arrive at a settlement. Fact-finding may not be used in discipline or discharge cases where the municipal employer has a civil service provision for such cases. The costs of fact-finding are share by the parties.

If an agreement is reached in negotiations with a labor organization representing a majority of the employees in a collective bargaining unit, it must be reduced to writing, either in the form of an ordinance, resolution, or agreement. Strikes by public employees are specifically prohibited.

Between February 8, 1962, the effective date of the amended statute, and May 15, 1964, the WERB received 41 cases. The greatest number, 155, were election cases. The other 86 cases—in descending order—were 46 fact-finding, 25 mediation, 14 prohibited practice, and 1 arbitration. Fact-finding reports have been issued in 10 cases.

Labor organizations have been certified as the bargaining representative in the vast majority of representation elections, 99 out of 114, which have been conducted by WERB. WERB believes that most of the certifications confirm existing bargaining practices and do not necessarily represent any significant extension of public employee organization. Only labor organizations which have been certified or recognized by the municipal employer have the right to avail themselves of the fact-finding procedures.

Bargaining Unit Questions

Any bargaining representative chosen under the statute is certified as the exclusive collective bargaining representative for the purposes of engaging in conferences and negotiations with their municipal employer. (48) Section 111.02(6) of the Wisconsin Statutes defines the term "collective bargaining unit" to mean:

". . . all of the employees of one employer . . . except that where a majority of such employees engaged in a single craft, division, department or plant shall have voted by secret ballot as provided in Section 111.05(2) to constitute such group a separate bargaining unit they shall be so considered. . . ."

The section just quoted permits employees to determine their own bargaining unit if the proposed unit otherwise constitutes an appropriate unit under the statute—meaning a craft, division, department, or plant.

Craft and Professional Employees

The WERB has defined craft employees to include, "those persons who can be classified as a distinct and homogeneous group of skilled journeymen working together with their respective apprentices and helpers." (49) Professional employees are included within the definition of craft employees. On this basis, teachers have been certified in separate units. (50) The WERB has recently certified a unit composed of doctors and dentists employed by the city of Milwaukee. (51) The nurses employed by Milwaukee selected the Staff Nurses' Council of the Milwaukee Health Department, an affiliate of the Wisconsin State Nurses' Association, as their bargaining representative.

Supervisors

The WERB has determined that supervisors are agents of the municipal employer within the meaning of the statute and, therefore, cannot be included in the same collective bargaining unit as other employees. The WERB has made this determination although the statute does not specifically exclude supervisory employees from the definition of employees on the grounds that the inclusion of supervisory employees in the same bargaining unit as the employees whom they supervise would conflict with the supervisors' responsibility in performing their management functions. As agents of the municipal employer, their duties in directing the work force and maintaining discipline would interfere with the protected rights of employees to organize and to be represented by organizations of their own choosing. (52)

The WERB later ruled that mere membership of supervisors in a labor organization would not be prohibitive of the statute, but because supervisory personnel were members of, or held office in an employee organization, a suspicion could be raised that the labor organization was dominated by, or subject to, interference by the municipal employer. The number of supervisors among the membership of the organization and the ratio of supervisors to other members are factors to be considered in each case, as well as the question of whether supervisors hold office and participate in the formulation of bargaining policies and programs of the labor organization. (53)

The following factors have been considered in the exclusion of supervisors from the bargaining unit: pay differentials; level of supervision; number of persons supervised; and the authority of the supervisors to recommend hiring, firing, promotion, or transfer of employees. (54)

Name of Employee Organization

Any employee organization whose purpose is to represent municipal employees in conferences and negotiations with their municipal employer on questions of wages, hours, and conditions of employment is considered a "labor organization" and is thus entitled to use the statute regardless of what name the employees may use to describe their organization. (55) Various locals of the Wisconsin Education Association have been considered as labor organizations in elections conducted at Milwaukee, West Allis, Madison, and Janesville.

Prohibited Practices

The WERB has set aside the voluntary recognition extended by a school board to a local affiliated with the Wisconsin Education Association on the Ground that the activity of the superintendent of schools interfered with the rights of the teachers under the statute. The WERB found that the superintendent had unlawfully assisted the local education association in obtaining recognition on the basis of signed authorization cards checked by the school auditor. At the same time the superintendent had directed representatives of the local union, affiliated with the Wisconsin Federation of Teachers, to petition the WERB for an election if it wished to secure representation rights. The WERB ordered the school district to cease and desist from recognizing the local education association unless, and until, it had been selected as the exclusive collective bargaining representative. (56)

The WERB has also held that a school district, by the action of its principal in soliciting membership applications and dues and by selling tickets for the convention of the Wisconsin Education Association to the teachers employed by the school district, unlawfully assisted such organization and interfered with the rights of its employees to join or to refrain from joining a labor organization. (57)

The WERB has held that a county highway commissioner engaged in a prohibited practice by interrogating employees concerning their union activity, by requesting employees to work against union activity, and by discharging an employee because of his organizational activities on behalf of a labor organization. The county was ordered to reinstate the employee with back pay. (58) A similar ruling was made in the case of a county home because of its action in discharging a butcher. (59)

Fact-finding

In the event that the municipal employer and the recognized or certified labor organization are unable to agree on the terms of a collective bargaining agreement after a reasonable period of negotiations, they may be considered to be deadlocked and thus to have established a condition precedent to the appointment of a fact-finder. The fact-finder, who must be "a qualified and disinterested person," is authorized to hold hearings with subpoena powers, and is directed to make written findings of fact and recommendations for the solution of the dispute which shall be made public.

The WERB, however, is proscribed from appointing a fact-finder even though the conditions for fact-finding have been met, in the event that a local municipality has adopted fact-finding procedures substantially in compliance with the statute.

The Wisconsin League of Municipalities has suggested the adoption of local fact-finding ordinances providing that, in the event of a deadlock, the municipal employer and the labor organization should each nominate a representative to the fact-finding panel who would, in turn, attempt to agree upon a third. In the event that the parties were unable to agree upon a third fact-finder, the American Arbitration Association would be authorized to name the third party. The WERB has indicated that it would appear that such procedure would be in compliance with the Wisconsin statute. (60)

Budget Deadlines

The WERB has been presented with the question of whether a petition for fact-finding should be processed since the municipality's budgetary deadline had passed. The municipal employer argued that since the time for adopting the municipal budget had passed, no meaningful purpose could be served by fact-finding since no monies would be available to act upon the recommendations of the fact-finder. Therefore, the municipality did not have the capacity to negotiate further.

The WERB rejected this argument, concluding that the municipality had the statutory authority to make changes with respect to the compensation and the number of positions in municipal employment if it felt that such changes were desirable. The WERB recognized that the municipal employer would not be obligated to make such changes, but that it could do so if it wanted to adopt the fact-finders' recommendations. The WERB's memorandum stated that to adopt the argument of the municipal employer would encourage municipalities to hide behind the shield of budget procedures to thwart the operation of collective bargaining and would frustrate the legislative intent. (61)

Strikes and Fact-finding

The WERB has also been required to determine whether it would process a fact-finding petition during a strike by municipal employees, since Section 111.70 specifically prohibits strikes by municipal employees. The WERB has declared that it will not, in the absence of good cause shown, process a petition for fact-finding while a strike is pending:

"The Legislature, in adopting Section 111.70, authorized fact-finding with public recommendations as an aid in the resolution of municipal employer-employee labor disputes, and as a substitute for the strike weapon utilized in private employment. The Legislature recognized that employment policies in municipal employment should be determined largely as a result of reasonable persuasion and negotiation, rather than by pressures generated as the result of a strike. The fact-finding procedure set forth in the statute is designed to give representatives of municipal employees an opportunity to persuade the municipal employer and the public of the merits of their particular requests with reference to the wages, hours, and working conditions of the municipal employers. . . . We do not believe that labor organizations who ignore these considerations by engaging in a strike, should at the same time be entitled to the benefits of fact finding or other rights granted to them by the statute. The Board, as a general policy and in the absence of good cause shown, will decline to process any fact finding petitions filed by a labor organization which is engaged in a strike." (62)

Thereafter the WERB appointed a three-member fact-finding panel to hear cases affecting the Milwaukee Police and Fire Departments and the Milwaukee Department of Public Works. The proceedings, which are still pending, were combined under a statute which permits the WERB, in complex cases on the consent of the parties, to appoint three fact-finders.

The WERB further stated in its memorandum that the municipal employer had the primary duty and obligation to take action to terminate the strike, but that, in the event the municipal employer failed to take such steps, the WERB, if the public interest required it, would take whatever action was necessary to terminate the strike. Prior to the WERB's appointment of the fact-finders, the strike was terminated after the Milwaukee Common Council passed a resolution joining in the petition for fact-finding and expressing a "strong moral obligation . . . to give every consideration to any recommendation of a responsible fact-finder."

In determining whether the conditions for fact-finding have been met, the WERB has, in some cases, assigned an informal investigator to contact both parties to determine whether the conditions for fact-finding have been met. Such method can and has been used to mediate the dispute. In other cases formal hearings have been conducted. It has been the experience of the WERB, that only after a clear definition of the issues such as wages, seniority, insurance, or pensions, can a determination be made as to whether the parties are, in fact, deadlocked.

Have Fact-Finding Recommendations Solved Municipal Employee Labor Disputes?

As of May 15, 1964, 46 petitions for fact-finding had been filed with the WERB. Fact-finding petitions were withdrawn in a large number of cases prior to the appointment of the fact-finder for such reasons as these: The conditions for fact-finding had not been met; the dispute was resolved in mediation; the parties had indicated their desire to continue negotiations. Fact-finders were appointed in 15 cases.

The WERB conducted an informal inquiry to determine whether the fact-finders' recommendations, in the 10 cases in which such recommendations were issued, were accepted in toto, in part, or were rejected by the municipal employer. In six cases, the recommendations of the fact-finder were accepted or contributed materially to the final settlement. In two cases, the fact-finder's recommendations were rejected by the municipal employer apparently without any comment as to why such action was taken. In two recent cases, adoption of the fact-finder's recommendations is still under consideration by the municipal employer.

A fact-finder has recommended that the collective bargaining agreement be reduced to writing and that it should contain a grievance procedure with final and binding arbitration to determine grievances over the interpretation of the agreement. (63) Another fact-finder has stated that it is the duty of fact-finders to make a prediction of the probable results of free collective bargaining in formulating their recommendations. (64)

A strike of county highway department employees occurred because of the declination of the county board, by a narrow vote margin, to adopt the recommendations of the fact-finder. (65) However, after a one-week strike the recommendations were adopted by the county board when a WERB mediator suggested that five cents of a ten-cent recommended wage increase be made retroactive for two months less than had been recommended by the fact-finder.

Teachers' Case

The most recent fact-finding recommendations involved the Board of Education of the city of Eau Claire and the Eau Claire Federation of Teachers. The fact-finder recommended substantially higher salaries for career teachers than the schedule adopted by the Board. The fact-finder observed that it is in the public interest

". . . to give somewhat greater rewards to the career teacher who takes the trouble to better himself educationally and gives long years of service with attendant gains in experience, as compared with the younger teachers who do not make teaching a lifetime career. It is certainly in the public interest to offer inducements to qualified people to adopt teaching as a permanent career. Likewise there is much that can be learned only by experience." (66)

In this case, the recommendations were accepted by both parties after slight modifications.

Arbitration

In one case, pursuant to the terms of a collective bargaining agreement, the WERB named an arbitrator at the joint request of the city of Peshtigo and a local of the International Brotherhood of Teamsters. The issue involved was whether an employee was discharged for cause. The arbitrator held that the employee was improperly discharged because no written warning notice was served on the employee prior to the discharge, as expressly required by the terms of the agreement. (67)

In the arbitration proceeding the city challenged the validity of the collective bargaining agreement under which the arbitration was held for the following reasons: The contract expired on December 31, 1963; Section 111.70(4)(i) provides that agreements between municipal labor organizations and municipal employers shall not remain in effect for a period exceeding one year; the statute provides that such agreements shall be binding upon the parties only if express language to that effect is contained therein.

The arbitrator rejected this argument and concluded that the agreement to arbitrate, although contained in the contract, was also a separate agreement to submit a specific issue to an arbitrator for his determination. The submission agreement to arbitrate the discharge which occurred during the life of the contract was made after the contract had expired and without any objection on the part of the municipal employer.

The arbitrator relied on the decision of the U.S. Supreme Court in Enterprise Wheel & Car Corporation (68) which upheld an arbitrator's decision restoring an employee to employment even though the contract had expired because the submission agreement had conferred authority on the arbitrator to interpret the contract. Therefore his authority did not expire with the contract.

The arbitrator also cited a decision of the Wisconsin Supreme Court (69) which upheld the enforceability of agreements to arbitrate made by municipalities. This dispute arose over the terms of an employment contract with an architectural firm. The Wisconsin court relied on the provisions of Section 298.01 of the Wisconsin Arbitration Act, which is similar to the federal arbitration act and many state arbitration acts in that it does not apply to contracts between employer and employees. However, under a special section of the arbitration statutes, the WERB is authorized to name arbitrators.

144

It would thus seem that if agreements between municipal employers and labor organizations are considered to be contracts of employment within the meaning of the arbitration statutes, agreements to arbitrate grievances in municipal employment would not be enforceable under general arbitration statutes unless, like Wisconsin, there is an express provision. On the other hand, if contracts between municipal employers and labor organizations are not considered contracts of employment within the meaning of arbitration statutes, the agreement to arbitrate would be enforceable in the courts, as in the city of Madison case cited above. The city of Peshtigo complied with the above decision.

Authority of Arbitrators

There has been widespread belief that employee grievances in public employment may not be submitted to final and binding arbitration because such procedure would be an invalid delegation of legislative responsibility to fix the terms and conditions of employment. This conclusion makes no distinction between arbitration of disputes to determine fixed liabilities or rights under an existing agreement, and arbitration to initially determine the conditions of employment. The interpretations of the Wisconsin and Pennsylvania courts seem to be putting to rest the legal objections to arbitration of grievances.

A more serious argument as to unconstitutional delegation of power can be made over arbitration of the terms of a new agreement, but not if the arbitration is "advisory," and thus subject to the ratification by the legislative body. This, in effect, is what happens in the case of fact-finding with the public recommendation fact-finding procedure under the Wisconsin Statute. However, other statutes such as those of Rhode Island appear to provide for final and binding arbitration of the terms of employment for firemen and policemen.

It should be recognized that state legislatures can, and do, control some of the employment policies of local units of government. For example, states have teacher contract laws which govern the circumstances under which teachers can be hired or fired. Many state statutes provide minimum wage laws, retirement programs, and hours of work for local employees, particularly policemen and firemen. Since state legislatures can thus regulate local employment policies of their political subdivisions, it may be argued that it is constitutionally possible to provide for arbitration of public employee disputes over the terms of employment. Likewise, the matching fund program for many occupations, state and local, make it difficult to determine who is a state or local employer. This is particularly true of welfare programs.

Whether compulsory arbitration of the terms of employment would be good public policy is another question. Inherent is the danger that with arbitration readily available, public employers and public employee organizations might yield too easily to the temptation to let a third party settle their differences without first making a serious effort to resolve the dispute.

Developments in Municipalities

The developments which have been described above at the federal and state levels have been paralleled by many cities and counties throughout the country. Time and space will permit only a brief mention of their existence. A review of the experiences of the cities of Sacramento, Cleveland, Los Angeles, Hartford, Philadelphia, Detroit, and Cincinnati may be found in a 1963 study by the Public Personnel Association. (70) A detailed report of the New York City experience may be found in the annual reports of the American Bar Association, Section on Government Employee Relations.

Union Security Agreements

The question of the legality of union security agreements in public employment needs further study both as to its legal aspects and as to whether it is good public policy. While the check-off of dues is in practice in a number of jurisdictions, union security provisions are rare. An argument can be made that union security provisions are invalid because they establish a condition of hire which would be inconsistent with most merit systems. However, this argument might be overcome as to its legal objection by making the union security provision applicable only after the probationary period of employment had passed. This would be similar to the Taft-Hartley 30-day union shop provision.

Strikes in Public Employment

Strikes in public employment, though infrequent when compared to private employment, cause great public concern and, in some instances, possibly public hardship. A one-day strike in 1962 by school teachers in New York City and a four-day strike by school teachers in East St. Louis in May, 1964, brought dramatic public attention and gained increases for the Teachers Union of from $300 to $900 per year. Similarly, a two-day strike in May, 1964, by the Utah Education Association was in the national news. A two-week strike by garbage collectors in Milwaukee in November, 1963, received some public attention, while a strike of a county highway crew in Wisconsin in May, 1964, went nearly unnoticed.

The strikes in New York and Wisconsin were expressly prohibited by statute. No express statutory limitation existed in Utah or Missouri. The right to strike in private employment exists by statute. No such protection exists in public employment, with limited exceptions. A California court has construed the Los Angeles Metropolitan Transit Authority statute as creating the right to strike by implication since employees, in addition to being granted the right to organize and bargain collectively, were also given the right to engage in other concerted activities for the purpose of collective bargaining or other mutual aid or protection. (71)

Strikes Challenge Government Sovereignty

The reasoning behind court decisions and statutory prohibitions of strikes in public employment is simply that government will not permit a challenge to its sovereignty by the use of the strike weapon. This viewpoint has been summarized:

"Those who work for governmental bodies are deemed to have a higher obligation to refrain from interfering with its operations than does the ordinary citizen." (72)

This explanation makes more sense than attempts to justify prohibitions against strikes by public employees on the grounds of health and safety factors alone. For example, public hospital employees cannot strike, but employees of private hospitals can strike in many jurisdictions, including Wisconsin. Private utility workers may strike in any jurisdiction, but not so in the case of publicly-owned utilities. Strikes have occurred with disturbing frequency by private employees at missile site installations, while federal employees on the same project cannot strike. Employees of a private contractor repairing or constructing a road can strike, but public highway maintenance crews cannot.

In all of these illustrations the threat to public health and safety is at least equally serious in the event that a strike should occur; but in the private sector it is necessary for the President to find that a national emergency exists before a major strike may be enjoined even for a limited period. (73)

The U.S. Supreme Court, in a decision which invalidated the Missouri public utility seizure statute because it conflicted with federal law, made the following observation which has significance as regards the authority of the state chief executive to deal with strike emergencies in public and private employment:

"It is hardly necessary to add that nothing we have said even remotely affects the right of a state to own or operate a public utility or any other business, nor the right or duty of the chief executive or legislature of a state to deal with emergency conditions of public danger, violence, or disaster under appropriate provisions of the state's organic or statutory law." (74)

Political and Economic Factors

Essentially, strikes in private employment are designed to bring economic pressure to bear in order to influence settlement. Increasingly, as the public interest becomes affected, political pressures are exerted to influence settlements in private employment. In the public sector, decisions affecting wages, hours, and working conditions of public employees are essentially political decisions, but again economic factors must be considered. Political persuasion, lobbying, the assemblying of fact and argument are the tools of bargaining used by public employers and public employee unions. Thus, the strike weapon is not normally an integral or vital part of the collective bargaining process in public employment whenever public employees become too frustrated with the political processes. For example, Utah teachers struck after the Governor rejected the recommendations for teacher salary increases which had been made by a special study committee he himself had appointed.

Enforcing No-Strike Legislation

It is interesting to note that the states which have adopted no-strike legislation with stiff fixed penalties have rarely invoked such penalties, for the simple reason that it is impractical to discipline or discharge an entire work force. No-strike legislation in some states has been accompanied by the creation of affirmative rights on behalf of public employees to join labor organizations.

Recent statutes, such as those of Wisconsin and Oregon, have emphasized the creation of public employee rights and procedures for collective bargaining, while at the same time also banning strikes in public employment. If the no-strike ban is considered a quid pro quo for employee rights to collective bargaining in public employment, it appears to be a good bargain for public employees, for it amounts to a trade of a nonexistent right.

The experience of no-strike statutes has not been effective in banning all public employee strikes. There is some evidence that statutes with fixed and harsh penalties have created contempt for the law rather than respect. This is certainly one explanation for the modification of the Condon-Wadlin Act in New York and the prospect of further modifications after the Study Committee Report in 1965.

This statement should not be construed as an argument against public employee strike prohibitions in state or local ordinances or against the existing strict federal statute. Rather, this statement suggests that the public employers should fit the punishment to the offense, much in the manner that private collective bargaining agreements, 94 per cent, contain provisions for the arbitration of grievances arising over the interpretation of the agreement. (75)

Most of those same contracts contain no-strike clauses, the violation of which subject employees or their representatives to penalties. However, private employers do not discharge an entire work force for violation of a no-strike clause. They do discharge or discipline the ring leaders or persons guilty of gross misconduct and give others a lesser penalty.

Generally such measures have proved effective in private employment in curtailing wildcat strikes. However, some public employers, because of inexperience or political pressures, are not always as willing or as able to effectively discipline employees who engage in strikes or other misconduct.

It has been said that—

"Government which by statute or otherwise denies its employees the right to strike,—no matter how just might be the grievance, owes to its public servants an obligation to provide working conditions and standards of management-employee relationships which would make unnecessary and unwarranted any need for such employees to resort to stoppage of public business." (76)

Outlook for the Future

The events of the past nine years since that report was written show evidence that governmental units at all levels are increasingly recognizing and fulfilling those obligations by providing statutory protection for the organizational and collective bargaining activities of its employees. There is every reason to believe that many more states and municipalities will join the pioneering efforts of other states and municipalities in extending collective bargaining to its public employees. It is to be hoped that public employee organizations will recognize their responsibilities which have grown with their achievement of rights.

Good faith bargaining is a two-way street. The public employee union which makes a settlement at the bargaining table should not attempt to improve on the terms of the bargain before the legislative body when the bargain is up for ratification. Likewise, the public employer representatives must learn to live with commitments and not renege on promises to recommend acceptance of good-faith tentative settlements to the legislative body. The future will tell whether the extension of collective bargaining to public employment will be accompanied by mature and responsible conduct on the part of public employers and public employees.

REFERENCES

1. Daniel H. Kruger, "Trends in Public Employment," i.. Proceedings of the 14th Annual Meeting (Madison, Wis.: Industrial Relations Research Association, 1961), p. 354.

2. Monthly Labor Review, 1960.

3. American Bar Association, Second Report of the Committee on Labor Relations of Governmental Employees, 1955, p. 125.

4. Federal Register, May 23, 1963, pp. 5127-32.

5. For a detailed report and analysis of the federal program, see Report of the Committee on Law of Government Employee Relations of the Section of Labor Relations Law, Chicago: American Bar Association, July 30, 1963; also see Wilson R. Hart, "The U. S. Civil Service Learns to Live with Executive Order 10988: An Interim Appraisal," Industrial and Labor Relations Review, January, 1964, pp. 202-20; John W. Macy, Jr., "Employee-Management Cooperation in the Federal Service," in Management Relations with Organized Public Employees, Kenneth O. Warner, ed. (Chicago: Public Personnel Association, 1963), pp. 204-18.

6. Act No. 720, Public Acts of 1953, Alabama; Arkansas, Act 30, L. 1957; Georgia, Code Ann. 54-909, 54.9923 (1961); North Carolina Gen. Stat. 95-97-95-100 (Supp. 1959); Virginia Code 40.65-40.67 (1950).

7. Op. Eng. v. Water Board, 55 L.R.R.M. 2950, April 9, 1964.

8. Alaska, Ch. 108, L. 1959.

9. Potts v. Hay, 318 S.W. (2d) 826 (1958).

10. Government Code, Sec. 3500-3509, Ch. 1964, L. 1961; Sec. 1960-63.

11. Fellows v. La Tronica, Colo. Sup. Ct. 1962, 377 P (2d) 547, 52 LRRM 2386.

12. Act 495, L. 1963.

13. Norwalk Teachers' Association v. Board of Education, 83A (2d) 482 (1951). See Annot. 31 A.L.R. (2d), 1142 (1953).

14. Florida L., Sec. 839.221 (1957).

15. Atty. Gen. Opinion, March 18, 1959.

16. Metropolitan Transit Authority Act, Illinois L. 1945.

17. Atty. Gen. Opinion, August 16, 1961.

18. Atty. Gen. Opinion, January 9, 1963.

19. Ch. 670, Maryland L. 1961.

20. Mugford v. Mayor and Council, 44 A (2d) 745, 1945.

21. Mass. Ann. Laws, Ch. 40, Sec. 46, 1960.

22. Art. IV, Sec. 48, Mich. Const.

23. Act 336, Michigan L. 1947; also see Parker, "Role of the Michigan Labor Mediation Board in Public Employee Labor Disputes," Labor Law Journal Vol. 10, 1959, pp. 632-33.

24. Minn. Laws, Sec. 179.51-179.58; in re. Richfield Federation of Teachers; Minn. Supreme Court, 1962, 115 N.W. (2d) 682, 50 LRRM, 2399.

25. Art. I, Sec. 29, Mo. Constitution; City of Springfield v. Clouse (1947), 356 Mo. 1239, 206 S.W. (2d) 539.

26. Benson v. School District No. 1 of Silver Bow County (1959), Mont. Sup. Ct. 344 P. (2d) 117; 39 L.C. 66, 148.

27. Ch. 278, New Hampshire L. 1963.

28. Manchester v. Manchester Teachers' Guild (1957), 131 A (2d) 59, 32 L.C. 70, 622.

29. Art. I, Sec. 19, New Jersey Const.

30. Atty. Gen. Opinion No. 59-90, July 31, 1959.

31. Art. I, Sec. 17, N.Y. Const.; Erie County Water Authority v. Kramer (1955), 143 NYS (2d) 379, 28 L.C., 69, 463.

32. Sec. 601-605, Ch. 554, New York L. 1962.

33. S. Pr. 4557, New York L. 1962.

34. Board of Higher Education Resolution, January 23, 1964.

35. Sec. 95-85, 95-88, Ch. 742, North Carolina L. 1959.

36. Ohio, Sec. 4117.02-.05.

37. Ohio, Sec. 717.03.

38. Ch. 579, Oregon L. 1963 effective September 1, 1963.

39. Sec. 215.1-215.5, P.L. 1183, Pennsylvania L. 1947; Pittsburgh City Fire Fighters, Local 1 v. Barr, 408 Pa. 325 (1962), 50 LRRM 2894.

40. DeBlasia v. Capra, 55 LRRM 2110 Pa. Sup. Court, Western District, January 7, 1964.

41. Ch. 178, Rhode Island L. 1958.

42. H.B. 1342, Rhode Island L. 1963.

43. City of Pawtucket v. Pawtucket Teachers Alliance, 141 A (2d) 624, 34 L.C. 71, 545.

44. Levasseur v. Wheeldon, 112 N.W. (2d) 894, 49 LRRM 2525 (1962).

45. Texas, RCS 5154 C-1-4, 6; Dallas Independent School District v. A.F.S.C.M.E., Local 1442 (1959), 39 L.C. 66, 173; Beverly v. City of Dallas, 292 S.W. (2d) 172 (Ct. Civ. App. Tex., 1956).

46. Ch. 28, Sec. 1, Washington L. 1963.

47. Atty. Gen. Opinion, November 19, 1958.

48. Richland Center Utility, Dec. No. 5980, May, 1962; references are to WERB decisions some of which are reported by CCH Labor Reports and B.N.A. Labor Relations Reporter.

49. Winnebago County Hospital and Pleasant Acres Home, Dec. No. 6043, July, 1962.

50. Milwaukee Board of Vocational & Adult Education, Dec. No. 6343, May, 1963.

51. City of Milwaukee, Dec. No. 6252 D & F, April, 1964.

52. City of Wausau, Dec. No. 6276, March, 1963.

53. West Allis-West Milwaukee School District, Dec. No. 6544, November, 1963.

54. Lincoln County, Dec. No. 6200, January, 1963; Clark County, Dec. No. 6268, March, 1963.

55. Milwaukee Board of Vocational & Adult Education, Dec. No. 6343, May, 1963.

56. West Allis-West Milwaukee School District, Decision No. 6544, November 11, 1963, supra 9.

57. Joint District No. 1 of the Village of Waunakee, Dec. No. 6706, April 15, 1964.

58. Green Lake County, Dec. No. 6061, July, 1962.

59. Rock County Home, Decision No. 6655, March, 1964.

60. Shawano County, Dec. No. 6388, June, 1963, Supra 22.

61. City of Racine, Dec. No. 6242, 6242 A, March, 1963.

62. City of Milwaukee, Department of Public Works, Dec. No. 6575-B, December 12, 1963.

63. Fact-finding Recommendations, Shawano County, E. L. Wingert, October, 1963.

64. Fact-finding Recommendations, City of Racine, Philip Marshall, October, 1963.

65. Fact-finding Recommendations, Pierce County, Dave Johnson, February, 1964.

66. Fact-finding Recommendations, Board of Education, Eau Claire, E. L. Wingert, May, 1964.

67. City of Peshtigo, December No. 6613, May, 1964.

68. 363 U.S. 593, 1960.

69. 20 Wis. (2d) 361, 1962.

70. "Management Relations with Organized Public Employees," Kenneth O. Warner, ed. (Chicago: Public Personnel Association, 1963).

71. Los Angeles Metropolitan Transit Authority v. Brotherhood of Railroad Trainmen, 54 Cal. (2d) 684, 355 P. (2d) 905.

72. Illinois Legislative Council, Public Employee Labor Relations, 1958.

73. Labor Management Relations Act, 1947. Title II, Section 206, 61 Stat. 155, 29 U.S.C., Section 176, 1958.

74. Division 1287 v. Missouri 374 U.S. 74, 53 LRRM 2394, 2398.

75. Vol. 2, Collective Bargaining Negotiation, B.N.A. 51:7, 1960.

76. American Bar Association, Second Report of the Committee on Labor Relations of Governmental Employees (Chicago: The Association, 1955), p. 9.

13.

Shall We Bargain Away the Merit System?

Muriel M. Morse

Perhaps at no other time will we have as good an opportunity as we now have in the field of collective bargaining to assess the definite trend and pattern that has been emerging—and to make changes if changes are desirable.

Many public administrators have been tranquilized by the Rooseveltian concept that collective bargaining, as it exists in industry cannot be transplanted into public service; that the right to strike is opposed to the public interest; that a union shop is not compatible with a merit system. And so we have deluded ourselves into proposing a different definition for collective bargaining in government.

Collective bargaining in industry is described as requiring two adversaries of equal strength and authority bargaining in good faith, resulting in a written contract equally binding on both parties, and granting to employees the right to strike, other means of economic enforcement, and security of a union shop. On the other hand, public administrators in discussing this problem, and even in reporting in the literature (PPA's 1963 publication "Management Relations with Organized Public Employees" is a good example) have generally tended to accept a definition of collective bargaining as a method whereby representatives of the union and the employer negotiate, perhaps informally, but without most of the economic sanctions cited above.

The events of the past few years make it abundantly clear that we cannot have collective bargaining under a definition of our own choosing. Unlike Humpty Dumpty, we cannot say "when I choose a word, it means exactly what I choose it to mean—no more no less."

Changing Picture Observed

Tailor-made concepts of collective bargaining for the public service are unrealistic over the long run. They have occurred simply because we have been some 20 years behind the experience of industry in the use of this procedure. Events are changing that picture rapidly.

In an article in Challenge, November, 1961, Dr. Irving Bernstein, Professor of Political Science, University of California at

Los Angeles, points out that the American Federation of State, County, and Municipal Employees is the fastest growing union in the country next to the operating engineers. The drive to organize government employees has picked up speed since that time. Reasons cited for this growth include a narrowing of historic fringe benefits differentials between government and private industry, the growing variety in public employment, and the increased willingness of public agencies to experiment with collective bargaining. These experiments are bringing all of the weapons of the agreement into government.

In 1960, the Western Regional Director of the American Federation of State, County, and Municipal Employees described the scope and activities of union growth in a study made by the San Francisco Bay Area Chapter of PPA as follows:

"We have in our organization 302 local union agreements in 310 locals in 35 states and Canada. We have 209 bilateral contracts in 27 states and Canada. . . . We have 130 agreements granting the union exclusive bargaining rights as the bargaining unit. We have four union shop contracts in 59 agreements. We have maintenance of membership in 11 agreements. We have preferential shop agreements in two states. We have 103 agreements providing for arbitration."

In appearing before the California Assembly Committee on Industrial Relations, a few years ago, Dr. Bernstein testified that:

"The Metropolitan Transit Authority Act passed by the California Legislature in 1957, setting forth an experiment in collective bargaining, while not characterized by perfect smoothness, nevertheless was being carried forward successfully."

Part of that carrying forward was confirmation by the courts that, with the law silent, the strike was an integral part of this collective bargaining contract.

Also commented upon at that time were two interesting legal opinions of the State of Washington. The first was to the effect that a county may enter into a contract providing for a union shop. The Attorney General stated he could find nothing in the State Constitution, public policy, or statute law that would prohibit such a contract. His reasoning was that since the County Board of Commissioners enjoyed the right to select and hire employees, it was also free to require union membership as a condition of employment in the selection process. The same Attorney General also ruled that a school district might legally enter into a written collective bargaining agreement, because the power to employ embraced the authority to enter into contracts with employees either individually or collectively.

155

Modified Closed Shop Agreed On

The Philadelphia story is another example of "the weapons picture." Some experts maintain that collective bargaining in government does not necessarily involve formal negotiation or contract, and may consist of no more than discussion, conference, and negotiation; it does not work this way in Philadelphia. After a long history of negotiations with unions, and collective bargaining agreements on a year-to-year basis, Philadelphia finally embraced a form of its present contract in 1953. In 1959 employees were required to have union membership. A modified union shop with exclusive bargaining rights for a substantial segment of city employees was established. New employees in those classifications are now required to join the union within six months of appointment.

Philadelphia is not alone in this experiment. Exclusive bargaining rights are granted the union in 65 of their agreements with cities, the American Federation of State, County, and Municipal Employees reports. Indeed, the alternative to it, that is, multiple representation, or the job of bargaining with each recognized union or employee organization, is one on which many labor relations experts have commented in terms of loss of efficiency.

Settlement by Arbitration Gains

A third weapon, the settlement of disputes through arbitration, is progressing nicely in the public service. The 1961 San Francisco Bay Area Chapter report on collective bargaining pointed out that the California Conciliation Service had intervened in 56 labor disputes in the public service from 1947 to 1959. Incidentally, educational institutions and school districts were involved in the highest number of disputes served, and 21 labor unions and employee organizations were involved. Seven work stoppages occurred—five on the campuses of the University of California, and two others involving a city and a county in California.

For many years, the question of whether a public agency has the right to turn over to someone not responsible to the electorate certain decision making inhibited its use. Recently, however, there has been a tendency to view the use of arbitration as a good offices-type of approach in government where the arbitrator seeks a compromise and makes a recommendation to the final authority. At least 103 of the agreements reported to the San Francisco PPA Chapter study mentioned above by the American Federation of State, County, and Municipal Employees provide for arbitration. Where recommendations are universally upheld, de facto delegation has occurred.

Ultimate Weapon—the Strike

The ultimate weapon of the union is, of course, the strike. And here is where I think we have deluded ourselves perhaps most obviously. In an effort to get legislation approved which will permit collective bargaining in public agencies, proponents are all too willing to write in a no-strike clause. Strikes, although prohibited by law in the federal government and in many of the states, have occurred and are still occurring. This is true even when the so-called right to strike is prohibited either by law or by the terms of a collective bargaining agreement.

Sterling Spero, in Government as an Employer points out that a no-strike policy for civil service unions is a policy of expediency rather than any recognition of the moral force of the claims of government as an employer. H. Eliot Kaplan in The Law of Civil Service agrees that it does not answer the problem of preventing strikes by government employees simply to outlaw strikes. Leonard D. White philosophizes that strikes should be prohibited only where such action could bring direct and serious danger to a community; namely, the consequence of the strike upon the public interest. To follow this thinking is to find oneself in an impossible tangle of definition.

Collective bargaining has made headway in police and fire services which use the no-strike pledge required by the American Federation. But if permission to strike is based on the nature of the employment rather than the violation of government's sovereign authority, it can cause hardships if carried out.

For instance, a police force cannot function effectively without its communication facilities. Yet, the nature of the telephone operator's job is judged the same in public service as it is in a private public utility or corporation.

Substitute Collective Bargaining?

The point of this commentary is simply that our concerns as public administrators should relate to the whole gamut of collective bargaining and the weapons which are used to enforce it. Industrial practices for making unions effective are present in the public service, and it is logical they should be. The changing face of management-employee relations in government proposes to substitute collective bargaining, and the means to enforce it, for the merit system. This is the fact we must face, and it brings some items of concern to most merit system administrators. I should like to list them.

1. <u>Union Membership</u>. The right of an employee to join an organization of his choice and to be represented by that organization goes unchallenged. But in government there is a concept of an equal right, and that is a right not to join. Public jobs are distinguished from private employment in the concept of equal opportunity of all the citizens to compete for those jobs. The right of a county cited earlier to hire only workers who belong to a union flies in the face of this principle.

Furthermore, it is scarcely farseeing to say that while the closed shop might be a violation of the merit principle, the open shop is not. The very fact that someone must join a union in order to become the employee of a particular jurisdiction, limits recruitment. As a public service is entitled to the best without regard to race, creed, or color, it is equally entitled to the best without regard to any affiliation. The concept of equal opportunity for public jobs is certainly not compatible with the weapon of collective bargaining, namely, the union shop.

2. <u>Selection for Promotion</u>. The right to compete for public jobs has also been extended in most agencies to competitive promotion. The security found in the industrial union shop which provides for assignment by seniority, bidding for better jobs by seniority, and promotion by seniority, is quite opposed to many of the tools of the merit system. When we are talking on the one hand about better incentives for employee performance and better measurement of such performance, we might remind ourselves that seniority, not competition, is a corollary of collective bargaining.

3. <u>Determination of Wages and Benefits</u>. Another function of most merit system administrators is to provide information on wages and fringe benefits. If these are to be determined by collective bargaining, the prevailing wage theory goes out the window. A comment on the Philadelphia story is again in order here. Foster Roser reports that a major difficulty of collective bargaining in Philadelphia is that with no money, management can only negotiate on non-monetary terms, usually involving minor fringe benefits. A similar difficulty has recently been reported in Cincinnati, Ohio. Any personnel administrator faced with recruiting the best people he can for his jurisdiction would prefer being able to offer employees prevailing wages for comparable work. As a matter of fact, this system is more fair to all employees and to the citizen than it would be to go, for salary, to the group which can bargain best.

4. <u>Right of Individual Petition</u>. In representative government, it is generally conceded any individual employee has a right of petition, is entitled to speak for himself, and to use a counsel of his own choice in matters that affect his own welfare. If the efficiency of collective bargaining is achieved through exclusive recognition,

or if representation can be accomplished only through a group, then there is a destruction of this concept. At a time when we are so concerned with retaining the benefits of an individualistic society as well as its responsibilities, it would seem that the right of representation of more than one group is equally fundamental to a merit system in representative government. It is so fundamental that it has been the great practical deterrent to collective bargaining legislation in California.

5. Delegation of Responsibility. Also fundamental is a means whereby elected officials are held accountable for their decisions. There is a growing tendency to degrade this concept of sovereignty by saying that elective officials delegate many of their acts, and the signing of a collective bargaining agreement is no different from any other delegation. I submit that there is a difference when public officials can abdicate their responsibilities in a matter usually involving over 80 per cent of the public's money in an operating budget saying they are helpless to act because of commitments made in collective bargaining agreements.

6. Difference Between Government and Industry. If we go back to our original definition of collective bargaining, requiring two adversaries of equal strength and authority to bargain in good faith, then the structure of management in public service presents a difficulty. In industry, levels generally are clear cut, and supervisory workers excluded from the union. The public service, on the other hand, is far from clear cut on this score. The fact is that all public employees work for one boss—the citizen. Membership which would provide a balance of power is difficult to achieve since the citizen cannot be at the bargaining table.

7. Effect of Politics. Another concern of public agencies is the extent of political activity of its employees. In an article titled "Labor's Power in American Society," in California Management Review, Spring 1962, Dr. Irving Bernstein urges more political activity on the part of labor unions, more education of membership for active political participation, supplying funds to candidates in behalf of issues which labor supports, and, where this is useful to help in running campaigns.

A tradition of the American scene at the local level has been the nonpartisan nature of government. I think most of us would agree that nonpartisanship has helped the merit system to flourish. If labor takes a greater part in the political picture, then we must surely expect partisan political activity on the part of merit system employees. This is inevitable if labor's part includes a large segment of state and local government employees represented by single bargaining agents with national affiliation.

Confirmation of this is found in a news-gram in the June 3, 1963 issue of U. S. News and World Report as follows:

"A new move in Washington is to be watched closely. It's a move to get employees of the vast Government establishment organized into unions.

"Checkoff of union dues has won White House approval. Unions of Government workers, assured of checkoff will be able to grow in political strength. Postal workers long have had such a political power.

"It's said that there is a law against political activity by government workers. Actually, this law is largely a dead letter. What politicians are beginning to see is the chance to build a highly powerful political machine around the millions of people in Federal Government employment."

8. Finally, the public personnel administrator's concern for the right of public employees to strike does not need to be labored. That it is inherent in the right to bargain is perhaps best expressed, apart from practice, by Dr. Arthur Bieriman, President of the AFL-CIO Teachers Union, in a statement made in San Francisco and printed in the San Francisco Examiner, December 13, 1959:

"It may be argued that the right to strike is implied in the right to bargain collectively. To this argument we make no reply. Whenever men organize to achieve a goal there is an implication that at great need they may act publicly and forcefully in defense of their rights as citizens and human beings. We feel that the right to strike is inherent, it is not a privilege. In extremity, whether legally or not, men strike."

Here we have a clear-cut admission from a representative of a public employees' organization that strikes occur not as a matter of law, not as a matter of type of work, not even as a matter of recognition on the part of employees of the public interest (as indeed the teachers' strike in Gary, Indiana, during the last week of May, 1963, confirmed), but rather as a right associated with collective bargaining.

Choice of Systems Necessary

To sum up, the decision is not where to draw the line. The decision is about two kinds of personnel systems. Which are we going to have? They are different. They employ different principles, and they have different concerns. We can no longer believe that we can be half collective bargaining and half merit system. This is well stated in an article in Public Management, May, 1963 issue, by Douglas Weiford, City Manager, Eau Claire, Wisconsin. It points up clearly that the decision we really must make is whether the personnel administrator and the merit system are to survive.

If we believe in the merit system, more effective alternative machinery must be encouraged in government-employee relations. Drifting into collective bargaining is no answer. Unless we are to sow the seeds of our own destruction, we shall have to choose. Then it's up to us to devise a better climate than we have now for management-employee co-operation, and make statements of policy more explicit. They should include and spell out proper grievance procedures, the right of employees to be heard, regularly scheduled opportunities for consultations with representatives of employee groups, good channels of communication, and the ingredients of a sound personnel policy that allows employees to make recommendations for its improvement. They must, and can, be compatible with the basic principle of the merit system, responsive to the public interest, and flexible to meet today's personnel needs.

A. Bibliography

Foreword

The following annotated bibliography deals particularly with the negotiation aspects of management-employee relations, and is intended as a supplement to the one appearing in Management Relations with Organized Public Employees, edited by Kenneth O. Warner, Public Personnel Association, 1963. It was prepared by the Library of the United States Civil Service Commission.

Bibliography

American Management Association, Inc. Understanding Collective Bargaining; the Executive's Guide. New York: the Association, 1958. 415 pp.

> Part 2, Getting ready to talk contract: Insuring adequate preparation, by Selwin H. Torff; Climate—key to effective bargaining, by Clive B. McKee; The negotiating teams: A, Make-up of the management team, by Fred D. Hunter; B, The other side of the table: a portrait of the union business agent, by Hjalmar Rosen and R. A. H. Rosen; C, Final authority and responsibility, by Monroe Berkowitz; A step-by-step guide to the preparatory process.

Bambrick, James J., Jr. and Marie P. Dorbandt. The Use of Bargaining Books in Negotiations. Management Record, Vol. 19, No. 1, April 1957, pp. 118-21, 143-45.

> Lists advantages of this orderly approach to bargaining, both before, during, and after negotiations. Provides examples of content of bargaining books which show mass of information gathered and collected.

Campo, Arnold F. A Collective Bargaining Check-List. Advanced Management, Vol. 14, No. 2, June 1949, pp. 73-75.

> Outlines conditions essential for effective collective bargaining as well as policies and procedures that should be followed by both management and labor in negotiating contract and living under the agreement.

Chruden, Herbert J. and Arthur W. Sherman, Jr. Personnel Management. 2nd ed. Cincinnati: South-Western Publishing Company, 1963. 725 pp.

   Negotiating the agreement, pp. 493-503. Covers such areas as preparation, sources of bargaining information, bargaining procedures and strategies. Follows this with a discussion of the bargaining process—opening negotiations, analysis and resolution of proposals, bargaining pressures and deadlocks, overcoming deadlocks. Final section deals with content of labor agreement.

Dartnell Corporation. "Negotiating a union contract." The Handbook of Employee Relations. 1st ed. Chicago: 1957. 1391 pp.

   pp. 207-222: Includes information on selection of negotiators, attitude toward union committee, conference procedure, written contract. Also outlines essentials of a union contract.

Davey, Harold W. Contemporary Collective Bargaining. 2d ed. Englewood Cliffs, N. J.: Prentice-Hall, 1959. 388 pp.

   Preparation for bargaining and contract negotiations, pp. 100-115. This chapter traces ". . . a variety of techniques and procedures used by management and union representatives in preparing for bargaining and in the actual negotiations themselves. No technique or procedure, however, can even be a substitute for good faith, intelligence, integrity, courage, and experience in the bargaining process. Bargaining remains an art rather than a science."

Dubin, Robert. Working Union-Management Relations; the Sociology of Industrial Relations. Englewood Cliffs, N. J.: Prentice-Hall, Inc., 1958. 291 pp.

   Of special interest in the chapter on "Collective Bargaining as a Power Process," is the discussion of typical stages in the actual negotiation of a union contract which are described and analyzed.

Flagler, John J. "Preparation for Negotiation." U. S. Department of Agriculture, Ideas . . . Employee-Management Cooperation. Washington: 1963, pp. 29-32.

   Discusses four major areas of concern: Drafting proposals, training negotiating committee, developing membership support, and determining strategy and tactics.

Frankel, Saul. A Model for Negotiation and Arbitration Between the Canadian Government and Its Civil Servants. Montreal, Canada: McGill University, Industrial Relations Center, 1962. 76 pp.

    Chapter II on "Negotiations," discusses who should represent the government-employer and the staff side, identifies questions which are negotiable, and examines negotiating procedures.

Fritz, Richard J. and Arthur M. Stringari. Employer's Handbook for Labor Negotiations. Detroit: Management Labor Relations Service, Inc., 1961. 210 pp.

    Partial contents: Chapter 2, How to prepare for labor negotiations; Chapter 3, Union negotiators and their devices; Chapter 7, Bargaining table guides for management; Chapter 8, The first meeting.

Mugridge, C. F. "Negotiating a Labor Contract." Practical Approaches to Labor Relations Problems. New York: American Management Association, 1945. pp. 41-48.

    Examines several important aspects of negotiating a labor contract, but points out that no one method is correct under all circumstances. Discusses selection of management's spokesman, getting ready for negotiations, counter-proposal, bargaining process, and contract phraseology.

Posey, Rollin B. "How to negotiate with labor unions." Public Personnel Review, Vol. 14, No. 1, January 1953. Chicago: Public Personnel Association. pp. 11-17.

    Comments that "Negotiation becomes a new and important technique in personnel relations" when employer and union exercise authority over personnel matters in negotiation conferences.

    A how-to-do-it article which concentrates on negotiation objectives, preparing to negotiate, and techniques of negotiation.

Randle, C. Wilson. Collective Bargaining Principles and Practices. New York: Houghton Mifflin Company, 1951. 740 pp.

    Partial contents: The parties to collective bargaining, pp. 146-160; Preparation for collective bargaining, pp. 161-188; The conduct of collective bargaining, pp. 189-210.

Slichter, Sumner H., James J. Healy and E. Robert Livernash. The Impact of Collective Bargaining on Management. Washington, D. C.: Brookings Institution, 1960. 982 pp.

 Chapter 30: Negotiation of union-management contracts, pp. 918-945. Considers such aspects as union and management representation in negotiations, liaison between negotiators and administrators, preparations for negotiations, and methods of negotiation.

Smyth, R. C. and M. J. Murphy. Bargaining with Organized Labor. New York: Funk & Wagnalls Company, 1948. 302 pp.

 Chapter 3: Preparing for collective-bargaining negotiations; Chapter 4, Negotiating the collective-bargaining agreement.

U. S. Civil Service Commission. Employee-Management Cooperation in the Federal Service; Basic Training Materials. Washington: U. S. Govt. Print. Off., 1962. 1 v. (Personnel methods series No. 15).

 Includes section on consultation and negotiation which makes suggestions for preparing for negotiations, selecting negotiating committee, role of spokesman and committee members, anticipating issues, and discussion with top management. Information on conducting the negotiating conference considers opening conference, outlining issues, maintaining cooperative relationships, and avoiding apparent impasses.

U. S. Department of the Navy. Office of Industrial Relations. Employee-Management Cooperation; Techniques for Conducting the Negotiating Conference. Washington: 1963. 37 pp. (NAVEXOS P2427).

 Practical guide to give administrators and management negotiators the necessary "know-how" for negotiating with employee organizations.

 Contents: Subjects appropriate for negotiation; Fundamentals of negotiation; Preparing for negotiation; Outlining the issues—use of caucus; Negotiating tactics and techniques; Post-conference activities.

Yoder, Dale. "Negotiation and Contract Agreement." Personnel Principles and Policies; Modern Manpower Management. 2nd ed. Englewood Cliffs, N. J.: Prentice-Hall, Inc., 1959. 599 pp.

 Outlines common practices in collective bargaining and

describes most common procedures by which the parties seek to carry out their collective bargaining policies.

First section defines negotiation, collective agreements, and contract administration; next section notes usual procedures by which both employers and unions prepare for negotiating sessions; third section is concerned with the setting and practice in actual negotiation process; and finally, a section is devoted to contract administration.

B. | Contributors

Arvid Anderson —

. . . is Commissioner of the Wisconsin Employment Relations Board. The three-member Board is responsible for administering the statute governing employee-management relations in municipal governments in the state. Mr. Anderson has written extensively in the field of employee relations in the public service. He received an L.L.B. degree from the University of Wisconsin and was admitted to the Wisconsin Bar.

Paul Berthoud —

. . . is Employee Relations Director, Ground Employees, at United Airlines. He received an L.L.B. degree from DePaul University and was admitted to the Bar of Illinois. Starting first in the labor relations section of the Pullman Company, Mr. Berthoud now has over 20 years experience in labor relations work in the transportation industry.

Robert K. Burns —

. . . has been Executive Officer of the Industrial Relations Center of the University of Chicago since the center opened in 1945. Prior to assuming his present position, he helped found two successful business enterprises and served as consultant to a number of companies. He did his undergraduate work at the University of Washington and took graduate study at the London School of Economics and his Ph.D. degree from the University of Chicago.

Lew Fay —

. . . is Personnel Director for the city of San Diego, California. He was educated at the California Institute of Technology and the University of California at Los Angeles. He managed several business activities before entering personnel work with the California State Department of Employment in 1940, and served as Assistant State Manpower Director for Southern California during World War II.

William W. Hotchkiss —

. . . is manager of the Economic Analysis Department, American Motors Corporation, a position he has held since 1960. Prior to that time he spent several years as manager of the Manufacturing Department of the Automobile Manufacturers Association. He has a bachelors degree from Wayne State University and a masters degree from the University of Detroit.

Theodore H. Lang —

. . . is Chairman of the City Civil Service Commission and Personnel Director of the City of New York, a position he has held since 1960. Prior to that he was Deputy Personnel Director of New York and has served in various capacities with the New York Personnel Department and the Board of Education. He holds a B.S. and M.S. (Educ.) from City College, an M.P.A. from New York University and a Ph.D. from New York University. Dr. Lang has received four awards for distinguished achievement in his field and is the author of numerous articles.

Richard Martin Lyon —

. . . has been an attorney since 1955 with Seyfarth, Shaw, Fairweather and Geraldson, a firm engaged exclusively in management representation. Mr. Lyon taught at the College of Business Administration, University of Notre Dame. He is a member of the Bar of Illinois, Indiana and New York, and holds a Ph.D. in Industrial and Labor Relations, conferred by Cornell University.

Raymond F. Male —

. . . is Commissioner of Labor and Industry in New Jersey, and was previously Director of Personnel for the New Jersey Department of Institutions and Agencies and Executive Assistant to Governor Meyner. Past president of the International Association of Governmental Labor Officials, he holds an M.A. degree from Princeton.

John E. Massey —

. . . is Director of Personnel of the Tennessee Valley Authority. He received a B.S. degree from the University of Alabama and did graduate work in industrial and labor relations at the University of Maryland and Cornell University. As a career employee of TVA, Mr. Massey has occupied progressively more important positions in the Division of Personnel since joining its staff in 1937.

Muriel M. Morse —

. . . has been Assistant General Manager of the Los Angeles City Civil Service Department since 1947. Prior experience includes several years as Teaching Assistant, first at Stanford University then at the University of California at Berkeley, and as lecturer in Public Administration at the University of Southern California. She received her M.A. degree at Stanford University. Mrs. Morse has written several articles for Public Personnel Review.

Foster B. Roser —

. . . has been Personnel Director of the City of Philadelphia since 1956. Prior experience includes twelve years as Personnel Director of Flint, Michigan. After World War II he worked in Tokyo for two years as member of a special task force developing and modernizing the Japanese National Civil Service System. He is a graduate of the University of Michigan. In 1959 Mr. Roser received the Public Personnel Association's Award of Merit for his work in rebuilding the Philadelphia personnel system.

Douglas G. Weiford —

. . . has held the position of City Manager of Eau Claire, Wisconsin for the past eight years. Previous positions were Training Director for the International City Managers' Association and City Manager and Assistant Manager in Virginia cities. He holds a masters degree in Government Administration from the University of Pennsylvania. He serves as a College Visitor for the Seasongood Fund and has written many articles on local government subjects including municipal labor relations.

Frank P. Zeidler —

. . . in his current capacity as Director of the Wisconsin Department of Resource Development, acts as advisor to the Governor and Legislature of Wisconsin on municipal affairs and urban problems. He was mayor of the city of Milwaukee from 1948 to 1960 and member of the Board of Directors of the Milwaukee Public Schools from 1941 to 1947. Mr. Zeidler has been active in the United States Conference of Mayors, the American Municipal Association and the League of Wisconsin Municipalities.